Introduction to Oracle

Basic Skills for Any Oracle User

Bert Scalzo, PhD.

To my past and present miniature schnauzers Ziggy and Max – the two most *wonderful* four-legged kids that any parent could ever have ☺

Bert Scalzo, PhD.

Introduction to Oracle

Basic Skills for Any Oracle User

By Bert Scalzo, PhD.

Copyright © 2010 by Texas Publishing.
All rights reserved.
Printed in United States of America.

Editors: Jeff Smith

All names known to be registered trademarks appear in this text as initial caps.

Oracle, Oracle7, Oracle8, Oracle8i, Oracle9i, Oracle10g and Oracle 11g are trademarks of Oracle Corporation.

ISBN: 1450508782
EAN-13: 9781450508780

TABLE OF CONTENTS

Acknowledgements 1
Preface 2
Chapter 1: Terminology 3
    Definition of Data 3
    Definition of Database 3
    Relational Databases 5
    Primary Keys 8
    Foreign Keys 10
    Schemas and Users 12
    Database Name 13
    Conclusion 13
Chapter 2: Preparation 15
    Database Architecture 15
    Client Install 18
    Client Configuration 20
    Database Versions 25
    Conclusion 26
Chapter 3: Connecting 28
    Native Connections 28
    ODBC Connections 32
    JDBC Connections 36
    Conclusion 39

Chapter 4: Database Objects 40
  Data Definition Language 40
  Tables 41
  Key Constraints 45
  Indexes 47
  Views 48
  Conclusion 51
  Syntax Charts 52
Chapter 5: Basic SQL 57
  COMMIT 57
  ROLLBACK 59
  INSERT 60
  DELETE 62
  UPDATE 66
  SELECT 69
  Conclusion 73
Chapter 6: Advanced SQL 74
  ORDER BY 74
  GROUP BY 76
  HAVING 80
  DISTINCT 81
  JOINS 83
  Sub-SELECT's 91
  Conclusion 100

Chapter 7: SQL Developer 102
    Install 103
    Connecting 104
    Browsing 106
    Querying 114
    Conclusion 118

Chapter 8: TOAD 120
    Install 120
    Connecting 121
    Browsing 123
    Querying 133
    Conclusion 137

Chapter 9: Microsoft Office 138
    MS Excel 138
    MS Access 147
    Conclusion 151

Chapter 10: Database Sandbox 153
    Installation 154
    Utilities 157
    SQL Developer 159
    Conclusion 160

Author Bio 161

Acknowledgements

I've been doing Oracle work for more than two decades, and much of what I've learned has come from other great people who were willing to share their knowledge. So rather than list a few folks and risk missing anyone, let me just say thanks to all those many people "along the way" who've helped me to learn so much. Of course, I owe a very special thanks to Oracle Corporation. To paraphrase Garret Morris as Chico Escuela on the old Saturday Night Live, "Oracle been berry, berry good to me." Finally, special thanks to my favorite writing cohort Jeff Smith, whose skills and patience always help to make my writing accurate, readable and useful.

With my sincerest thanks,

Bert Scalzo, PhD.

Preface

These days everything is more or less computerized, with self service via applications and the web making us all regular, mass consumers of data. Thus unlike days past where databases and those who worked with them were considered a specialty, now database access and work is now deemed quite common – in fact so much so that databases are simply regarded as a commodity. Hence more and more people, both technical and not, find themselves needing to access and work with data in Oracle databases.

This book is meant for specifically that audience – those people new to Oracle who either know the business or have some technical skills, and all of whom now find themselves thrust into the world of accessing and working with data in an Oracle database. This book seeks to collect all the basic or fundamental skills and knowledge necessary into one easy to read yet valuable reference book. My goal is simply to have this one book assist everyone to be successful with Oracle.

Chapter 1: Terminology

To begin working with an *"Oracle Database"*, we first must define what the words *"Oracle"* and *"Database"* actually mean. Then we will build upon that most basic vocabulary to add additional terms you're likely to hear – such as *"schema"*, *"table"*, and *"index"*.

Definition of Data

Data is an asset – in fact it's any companies' most valuable asset. You cannot effectively perform your business functions without the ability to comprehend and process that data. In fact much of what people typically think of as *"work experience"* is nothing more than knowledge of business data and processes.

Definition of Database

In business terms, a database is quite simply a warehouse or repository of your business' data. For example the company's customer and order information might constitute what it considers as its data or database. Another way to think of this is that the business data or database is nothing more than a snapshot of what your *"data at rest"* appears like (i.e. not in flux or being processed). Thus it is the nontechnical means by which the business both recognizes and comprehends its data.

In technical terms, database simply refers to the highly specialized computer software utilized to house, manage and access that business data. Some examples of database software include Oracle, IBM DB2, Microsoft SQL Server and Microsoft Access. These are simply tools for getting at your data. It's the data itself that is the item or asset of value. Databases such as Oracle are nothing than tools to work with that asset.

Where most confusion enters is that people will often equate the business concept with the technology used to implement it. It does not matter whether business' data assets are housed in simple files or database software, the business has a repository or database of data it needs to function. But many people will assume that when you say database that you mean the data assets are housed within such database software. Therefore the word *database*" has almost universally become synonymous with the tools' technology.

As such, you will often hear your companies' business databases referred to as something like the following: Our mission critical Oracle database for customers and their orders. But the truth is that the word Oracle is the least important part of that statement. Because the business could later re-implement that database in another database software technology – and then the data asset reference might instead read: Our mission critical Microsoft SQL Server database for customers and their orders. So don't let the software tool itself become the center of the universe. Remember that the software is simply how the business concept has been implemented at this point in time.

Relational Databases

So what then is a "*relational*" database? As you work with more technical people in your company, you are sure to hear this word. It is nothing magical, simply meaning that the database software organizes, accesses and presents your data as "*tables*". Think of a database table like a worksheet in Microsoft Excel, it has rows and columns. Sometimes you'll hear the rows referred to as records. That's it.

The reason that relational databases became so important is that they were the very first and only database software whose approach was more logical rather than physical. Older database technologies (e.g. hierarchical and network databases) were more technically or programmer oriented. That is to say that rows or records in one table pointed to any related rows in the same or different tables via a physical pointer – such as a file or disk drive address, as shown here in Figure 1.

EMPLOYEE

Name	Job	Department Pointer
John Smith	Clerk	X000FFFEE
Jane Doe	Clerk	X000FFFEE
Bill Becker	Manager	X000FFFEE
Joe Haskins	Clerk	X000FFFAA
Mary Mavis	Manager	X000FFFAA

Figure 1: Non-Relational Table

So in order to access the employees who work in the "*Accounting*" department, the database user would have to find that row in the department table and note its address, then retrieve the employee rows that pointed to that very same physical address for their department.

Whereas in relational databases all the row connections are performed via more logical values, namely human readable ones. Thus the very same employee table as a relational construct would be much easier to read as shown here in Figure 2.

EMPLOYEE

Name	Job	Department
John Smith	Clerk	Accounting
Jane Doe	Clerk	Accounting
Bill Becker	Manager	Accounting
Joe Haskins	Clerk	Shipping
Mary Mavis	Manager	Shipping

Figure 2: Relational Table

So in order to access the employees who work in the "*Accounting*" department one just needs to search based upon that very simple yet business meaningful reference. That's the beauty of the relational model: it separates the internal physical storage and connectivity aspects totally away from the user access approach.

In fact Edgar Codd (who pioneered relational database theory in the early 1970's) devised 12 key rules as to what constitutes relational database management systems. Of those 12 rules, we have now covered the first two most fundamental and highly critical rules:

- The Information rule: All information in a relational database is represented logically in just one way - namely by values in column positions within rows of tables.

- The Guaranteed Access rule: Each item of data in a relational database is guaranteed to be logically accessible by resorting to a combination of table name, primary key value, and column name.

It's this second rule that we need investigate and understand better – as it introduces the concept of keys.

Primary Keys

The primary key is defined as the column or combination of column values in a table that represent a unique or singular method for identifying or separating one business entity or concept from another. So if we're talking about customers it might be something as simple as a customer number, whereas for an order it might be the combination of the customer number making the order and the date of that order.

Note that the primary key is a business concept and its associated database rule, and not the internal mechanism used to enforce or guarantee that result. For that, the database needs indexes – which are nothing more than a tool for speeding up access to rows of data based upon their logical value and which can also be utilized to enforce or guarantee their uniqueness.

Let's look at the common phone book as an example. The primary key or business rule might be that no two persons can have the same phone number – thus the combination of the phone number and the person's name must be unique. As we scan the phone book we sort of just accept that fact – that is we don't need anything special to signify it. But now as we scan the phone book to quickly find a particular person's phone number, we use the index values on the top of the page – as we know that the peoples' names are ordered in alphabetical order and will fall between the top left and top right most listed index values.

So in database terms, we therefore have a primary key that says the combination of the person name and phone number is unique –

and internally requires an index to ensure it. Plus we might need an index for fast access on just the name. So the constraint and its internal index are to enforce a business rule or requirement, whereas an index by itself is merely a tool to speed up access to rows of data. This difference is critical – and one that generally confuses very many people using relational databases.

So in short here are the main differences between a primary key and an index:

- Primary Key
    - Business rule or Requirement
    - Always Unique
    - Permanent Fixture (Always On)
    - Requires an Index to Enforce
- Index
    - Used to Speed Up Data Access
    - Dynamic In Nature (i.e. can be Added & Dropped as Needed)
    - Unique or Non-Unique

Foreign Keys

The concept of a foreign key is tightly related to relational rule #2 – the guaranteed access rule. It's also one of the most important and

10 Introduction to Oracle

useful mechanisms for relating data – hence the name relational database. As shown here in Figure 3, the "*child table*" (i.e. employee) rows point logically to the associated "*parent table*" (i.e. department) rows via the foreign key column – which is simply the parent table's primary key column(s) copied as a logical pointer or reference column into the child table.

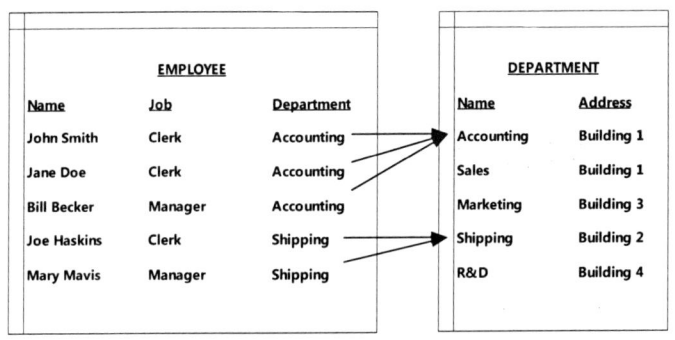

EMPLOYEE			DEPARTMENT	
Name	**Job**	**Department**	**Name**	**Address**
John Smith	Clerk	Accounting	Accounting	Building 1
Jane Doe	Clerk	Accounting	Sales	Building 1
Bill Becker	Manager	Accounting	Marketing	Building 3
Joe Haskins	Clerk	Shipping	Shipping	Building 2
Mary Mavis	Manager	Shipping	R&D	Building 4

Figure 3: Foreign Key

This foreign key construct enables us to "*join*" the parent and child tables (which will be more thoroughly explained in the later chapter on Structured Query Language or SQL). In essence this means that we can logically combine the parent and child data rows that are related as if that data was all just in one big row. So if we wanted a report showing the name, job and address for each employee – we could construct that by doing a join between employee and department and using the combined rows to obtain our required report values.

As with the primary key, a foreign key is a business concept and its associated database rule too, and not the internal mechanism used to enforce or guarantee that result. Once again indexes, in this case non-unique, are needed to both effectively and efficiently maintain these parent and child table data relationships. In fact for many database management systems the lack of a foreign key index can slow down the queries as you would expect – but also all operations on the parent and child tables due to complex row locking strategies required for the internal database processing.

It's worth noting that some databases don't offer foreign keys, and many applications built on top of relational databases that do lack foreign keys due to poor design. Since foreign keys simply implement business rules that you already know and live by, they are simply a mechanism to enforce what's supposed to be true. If they are missing, it might be time to see about adding them.

Schemas and Users

Not all database management systems have the basic concept of a schema. Oracle does. A schema is simply a database user account and all of the database objects owned by that user. Some database users own database objects such as tables and indexes, whereas others simply have the ability to connect to the database and then to look at other people database objects (if they've been granted access). You may hear the terms database schema and user utilized interchangeably. It's not uncommon to say schema when talking about object ownership and user when talking about connecting to the database (as in user id or user name).

Database Name

Every Oracle database has a unique identifier or name by which users reference it. You may hear it referred to by such names as database id, database name, global database name, Oracle instance identifier or Oracle SID. All of these equate to the same thing – the name by which you reference or point to the desired database. Think of this name like a phone number for the database, it's the reference name way by which you refer to or call it. You need to obtain this database name from your DBA as you'll need it for most real world work you'll attempt to perform.

Conclusion

In this chapter we reviewed the basic Oracle vocabulary that one should possess in order to understand how to work with their Oracle databases. Once you comprehend and appreciate terms such as data, database, table, primary keys, foreign keys, indexes, schemas and database names, you have all the requisites to work with most any Oracle database. Thus armed with this information you should never again feel like you're hearing worthless *"gobbledygook"* during any conversation about your Oracle database. You'll be in the know.

Chapter 2: Preparation

To successfully connect to and work with an Oracle Database from your Windows PC (desktop or notebook), there are several things that must be properly setup or configured. None of these are very complex, but failure to address these items can and will result in either problems, warnings and/or errors. So while this chapter may be brief, the basic concepts (and their mental images) are nonetheless very critical for your success. So it would be wise to read and learn this chapter's material well.

Database Architecture

The Oracle database itself will most often reside upon a server somewhere within your organization. While you can both run and access the Oracle database on most PC's these days, the raw performance, tight security and high availability requirements alone generally require a secure, centrally managed database server. Hence for most people your Oracle database will be on a server and have the 50,000 foot overall or high level architecture like that shown here in Figure 1.

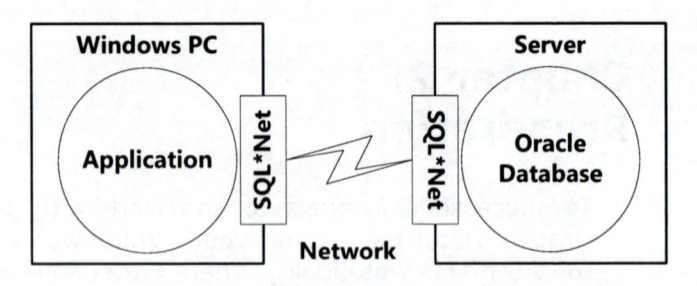

```
┌─────────────────────────┐         ┌─────────────────────────┐
│    Windows PC           │         │    Server               │
│         ╱─────╲   ┌──┐  │         │  ┌──┐   ╱─────╲         │
│        ╱       ╲  │SQL│ │         │  │SQL│  ╱       ╲       │
│       │Application│*Net├─┼──⚡──┼──┤*Net├─┤  Oracle  │      │
│        ╲       ╱  │   │ │         │  │   │  │ Database│     │
│         ╲─────╱   └──┘  │         │  └──┘   ╲       ╱       │
│                         │  Network          ╲─────╱         │
└─────────────────────────┘                    └──────────────┘
```

Figure 1: Database Architecture

The critical item of note is that both the client and the server need some supporting Oracle networking library files (often referred to as SQL*Net) in order for communication between your application and the database to occur.

Thus you must have those SQL*Net library files and network configuration files in place on your PC for database connections to function properly. Therefore most Oracle database users will have to perform a successful "*Oracle client*" install and configuration (covered later in this chapter).

Often the question gets asked "Why do I need to install the Oracle client as I simply intend to use Window's Open Database Connect (i.e. ODBC)?" The answer is actually quite simple – ODBC is merely a very generic Application Programmatic Interface (i.e. API) that standardizes the function calls to perform database actions, and not the network calls.

16   Introduction to Oracle

Thus the 50,000 foot overall or high level ODBC architecture looks like that shown here in Figure 2.

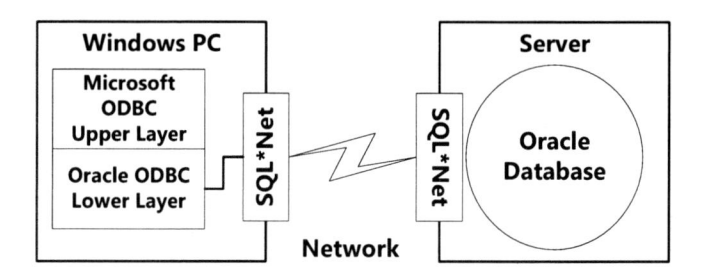

Figure 2: ODBC Architecture

This two layer architecture permits any application to call a consistent, single standardized set of upper layer ODBC function calls which then call the proper lower level layers for each database platform. Thus an application can be coded once and yet work with multiple databases. But once again, this does not handle the actual network connectivity. So the SQL*Net library files are still required – even when you're using ODBC.

There is one exception to these two high level architectures – and that's Java Database Connect (i.e. JDBC). JDBC does not require the Oracle SQL*Net layer on the Windows client as it inherently encapsulates and performs the communication aspects as well. You will often hear this referred to as the JDBC thin driver or JDBC thin client connection.

Client Install

The Oracle client installer is simply a Windows executable that functions like most other Windows application install packages. So you just download it and then run it – that's pretty much it.

There are three installer alternatives: the instant client (17-45 MB), the regular client (500-600 MB) and the whole enterprise database (1.7 GB). They are generally freely available at the following URL's:

http://www.oracle.com/technology/software/tech/oci/instantclient/index.html

http://www.oracle.com/technology/software/products/database/index.html

The instant client is the newest option and merely creates a directory where it installs the most basic required files. Oracle permits third party software vendors to distribute this bundle with their applications, so you may already have an Oracle instant client in place via some other application that you've previously installed.

The regular Oracle client and database installers run much more robust install packages that offer more choices and create a very special Windows registry area known as the "*Oracle Home*" as shown here in Figure 3.

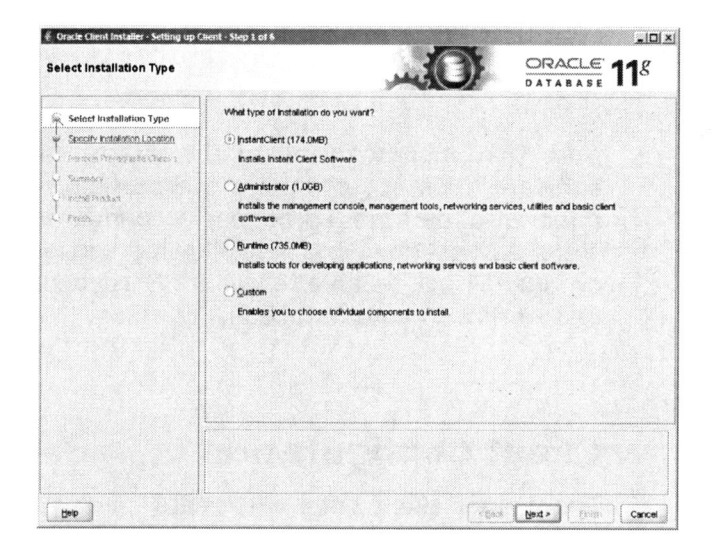

Figure 3: Client Installer

Notice that this client installer offers three choices: instant client (174 MB), administrator (1 GB), and run time (735 MB). The instant

Preparation

client here is a heavier, light-weight instant install (as it's three times the size of the basic instant client). The run time version adds most of the Oracle utilities or tools necessary to develop database applications (e.g. SQL*Plus). And the administrator choice adds "*DBA*" type utilities, including the management console.

Most people should install the run time client so as to get the basic database utilities and tools.

Note that merely installing the Oracle client software does not complete the process, you must also perform some basic configuration steps as described by the following section – or you will not be able to generally connect to and work with your database.

Client Configuration

The instant client does not create any special Windows registry entries or other environmental changes. So you have two tasks to perform to enable successful Oracle connectivity. First, you must create and define the **TNS_ADMIN** Windows environment variable as shown in Figure 4.

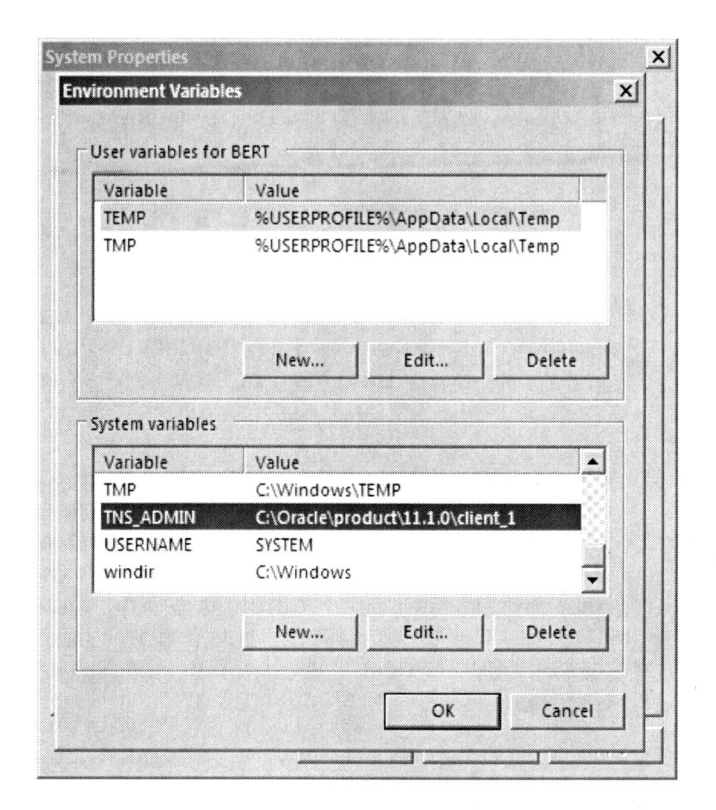

Figure 4: Windows Settings

This window is available on your PC via the "*System Properties*" pop-up dialog "Advanced" tab, via the "*Environment Variables*" button. Simply choose new or edit and point this to the directory where the instant client was placed.

Preparation

You also must add the Oracle client install directory with a "\BIN" suffix to your **PATH** environment variable. Here's an example:

PATH=%PATH%;%ORACLE_HOME%\BIN

That way when you ask to run an Oracle utility or tool that you do not have to fully qualify the file name every time. You do that here as well.

※ Remember that the regular client and database installers create a very special Windows registry area known as the "*Oracle Home*", so you do not need to perform these last two tasks. But regardless of the type of Oracle client installed, this next step is absolutely critical. It cannot generally be skipped.

※ In the directory where you installed the Oracle instant client or under $ORACLE_HOME/network/admin you (must) have a special text file named **TNSNAMES.ORA**. This special file is quite often provided either by your DBA or someone technical whose very familiar with that target database. The TNSNAMES.ORA file is very similar to the Windows HOSTS file, in that it allows you to use a database alias name such as ORCL to connect to your target database. Think of this alias like a telephone speed dial – you type this abbreviated name as shorthand

22   Introduction to Oracle

for the complete Oracle database connection information required. Figure 5 is an example of a simple TNSNAMES.ORA file.

```
ORCL =
(DESCRIPTION =
  (ADDRESS_LIST =
    (ADDRESS =
      (PROTOCOL = TCP)
      (HOST = 192.168.1.10)
      (PORT = 1521)
    )
  )
  (CONNECT_DATA =
    (SERVICE_NAME = ORCL)
    (INSTANCE_NAME = ORCL)
  )
)
```

Figure 5: TNSNAMES.ORA file

The HOST value can either be the IP address for the database server or an alias for that IP address defined in your Windows HOSTS file.

Failure to properly handle any of the above steps for either the instant or regular client

Preparation

configurations can result in Oracle an connection error message such as ORA-12154: TNS could not resolve the connect identifier specified. This particular error message simply means you provided a bad alias name, your don't have the TNS_ADMIN variable defined, or even possibly that your ORACLE_HOME registry entry does not point to the directory you think – thus you're referencing a TSNANEMS.ORA file that is incorrect.

The two easiest ways to avoid such connection problems is to either simply copy someone else's TNSNAMES.ORA file that is working or to run the Oracle Network Configuration Assistant (i.e. NETCA) utility. If you choose the latter method then you'll need to answer some local network IP address type information – so be prepared.

A very common reason you might run also into such connection naming errors or problems is if you can install multiple ORACLE_HOME clients on your PC. Then you need to manage those and set the default one using the Oracle Admin Assistant for Windows as shown here in Figure 6.

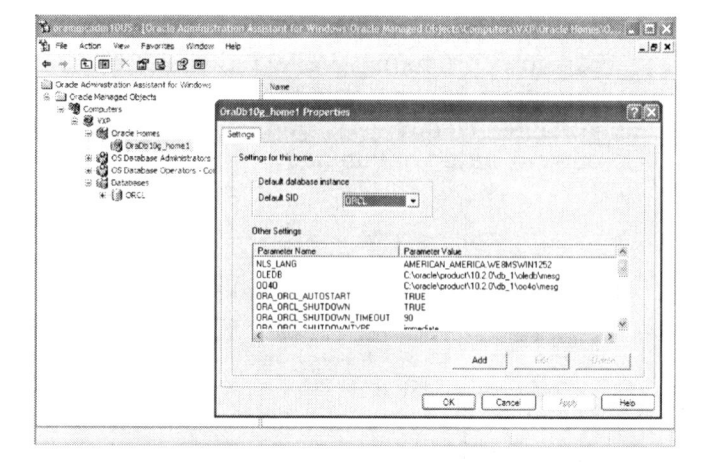

Figure 6: Oracle Admin Assistant

Database Versions

The Oracle database and clients, like most software, has different versions – such as Oracle 10g and 11g. These are simply the marketing names for the initial or base releases. The actual base or initial version numbers would be 10.2.0.1 and 11.2.0.6, for 10g and 11g respectively. In addition there are numerous patches available, and they are often named as follows: 10.2.0.7.

It is generally advisable that you use a client version that's the same or newer version than the database you connect to. So you should not use a 10g client when connecting to an

11g database. It will work, but you may well run into problems. In fact the simple rule of thumb is to just use the newest base client version available – and maybe up to the current patch minus one.

To verify which Oracle database version your server is running, it's best simply to ask your DBA. As for ascertaining your Oracle client version, the easiest way is simply to launch a SQL*Plus session and note what version the banner displays as shown here in Figure 7. Note that the first Oracle version line displayed is for your client and the second is for the database you've connected to. So you can actually ascertain both Oracle client and server versions this way.

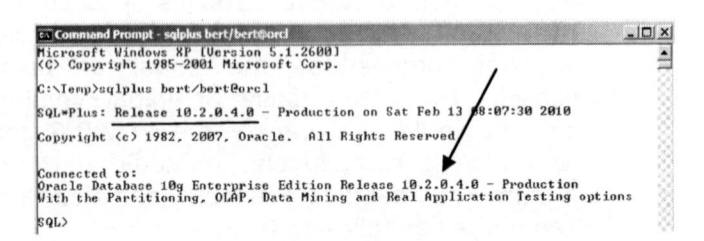

Figure 7: Oracle Client Version Check

Conclusion

In this chapter we reviewed the basic concepts and processes you need to understand and perform in order to begin successfully working with your Oracle databases. The contents of this chapter are critical and qualify as "*must know*" materials. It explains the basic Oracle database architecture, the client software installer options, plus the client configuration steps generally required for connecting to a database. You will not be successful with the rest of this book if these steps are not both properly completed and fairly well understood.

Chapter 3: Connecting

The first two chapters covered Oracle terminology and configuration issues that are prerequisites for successfully working with your Oracle databases. Now it's time to perform your very first Oracle database task – connecting to your database. That may seem like an anticlimactic task and you may wonder why devote an entire chapter to such a basic item?

Think of creating the database connection like making a phone call. If you don't have the proper equipment, a service plan, the number of whom you're calling and knowledge of how to dial that number, then you cannot initiate a phone call and thus cannot hold a meaningful conversation. The same is true for databases. You must successfully connect before you can retrieve, insert or update your data.

Native Connections

Recall from Chapter 2 the discussion about Oracle's client side library or SQL*Net, and its 50,000 foot view of the basic architecture shown here in Figure 1.

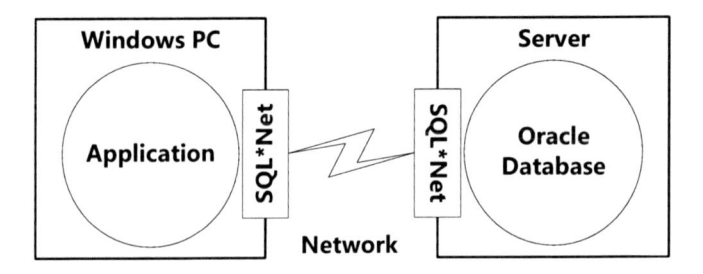

Figure 1: Database Architecture

When the application you're using to access your database talks directly to the Oracle SQL*Net library itself, that's called a *"Native"* connection. You may also hear this referred to as OCI or *"Oracle Call Interface"*, which is simply the name of that library's interface. So when your application makes direct calls to the OCI then you're performing a native connection – which many consider to be the most efficient or fastest connection method.

When you attempt to establish a native connection, you generally need three pieces of information: your user name, password, and the database name or SID of the target database. Some applications may also offer you the ability to over-ride the Windows registry setting for the default Oracle home (i.e. the location of the SQL*Net libraries and TNSNAMES.ORA file). As such you will often see a connection pop-up screen (or something similar) to the one shown here in Figure 2.

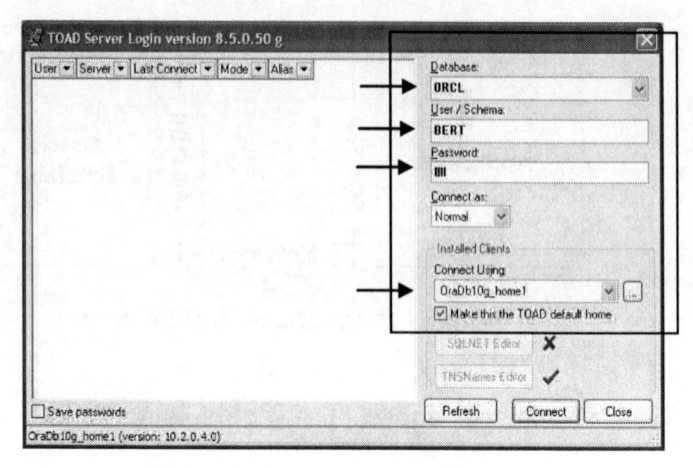

Figure2: Connection Screen

In the particular example I used Quest Software's popular *"TOAD for Oracle"* freeware, which you can download at http://www.toadworld.com/Downloads/tabid/60/Default.aspx. We will more thoroughly cover several other popular Oracle tools in a later chapter – including Oracle's SQL*Plus and SQL Developer.

But let's look at examples of creating native database connections using these two other tools now so that you have more than one example. Figure 3 and Figure 4 thus show creating both SQL*Plus and SQL Developer database connections respectively. Note that both of these Oracle tools will have been installed on your PC if you chose the *"run* *time"* Oracle client installation option as advised in back chapter 2.

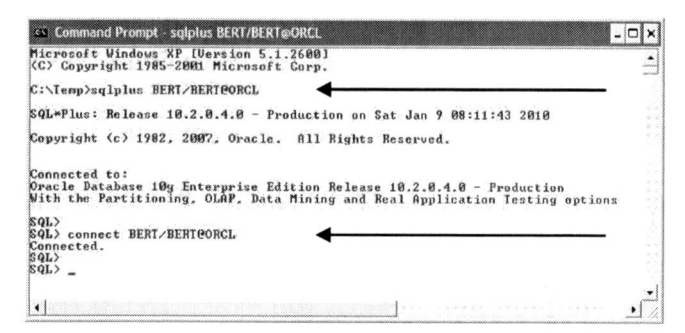

*Figure3: SQL*Plus Connection*

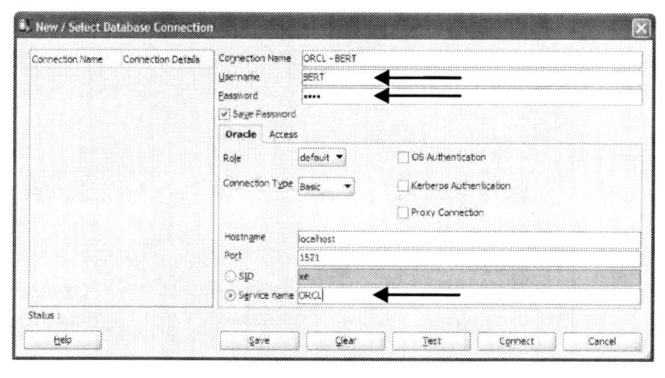

Figure 4: SQL Developer Connection

The key point is that native connection dialogs or screens will all look pretty much the same – and ask for those three pieces of connection information.

Finally, most database connections will operate in one of two modes: either they will persist until you manually terminate them (e.g. closing the application), or your DBA may have them set to automatically timeout (i.e. end) after a specified time of user inactivity. Thus if you get Oracle errors such as ORA-12170: TNS Connect timeout occurred, then talk to your DBA. That might be not be a problem per se, but rather database security policy enforcement.

ODBC Connections

Recall from Chapter 2 the discussion about ODBC connections still requiring the SQL*Net client installed, and its 50,000 foot view of the basic ODBC architecture shown here in Figure 5.

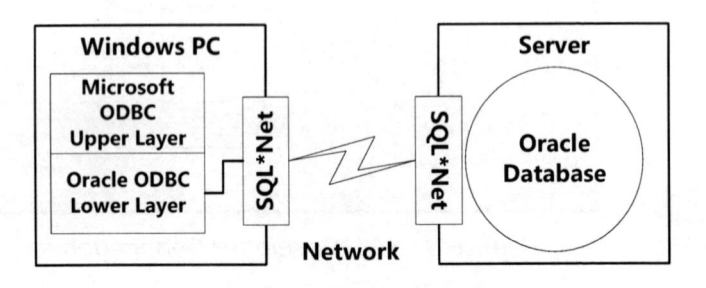

Figure 5: ODBC Architecture

ODBC database connections are pretty simple in theory, but they do require a little more work up front. Most applications that connect via ODBC will display an ODBC data source list to choose like shown here in Figure 6. Here I'm using Quest Software's *"TOAD for Data Analysts"* freeware, which you can download at http://www.toadworld.com/Downloads/tabid/60/Default.aspx. Unlike *"TOAD for Oracle"*, *"TOAD for Data Analysts"* can connect to almost any type of database platform – including Oracle.

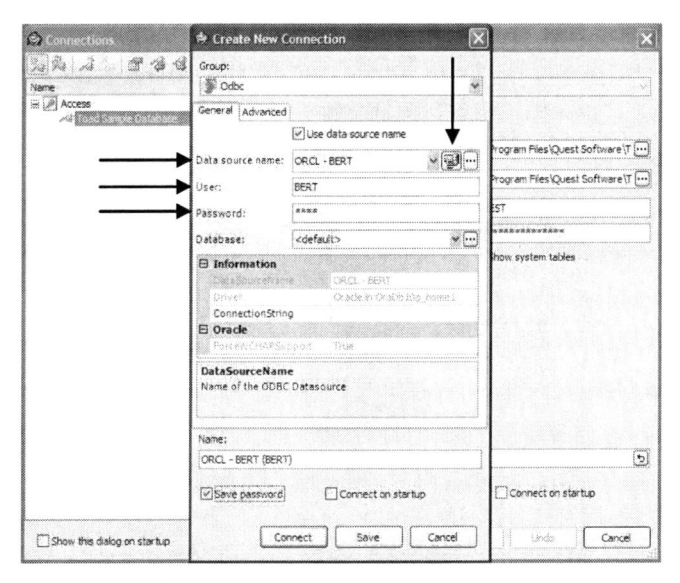

Figure 6: ODBC Connection

But where did this *"ORCL – BERT"* data source come from? How do you add new entries to this drop-down list? That requires you to use

Connecting   **33**

the Windows ODBC Administrator as shown in the next few figures. You can launch it either via the Windows Start Menu -> Administrative Tools, or most ODBC based tools will offer a button next to the drop-down list (like shown above) for creating new ODBC data sources.

When you first launch the ODBC Administrator you will see the main screen as shown in Figure 7 – don't be surprised if there are no predefined ODBC data sources. There are two types of data sources called data set names (i.e. DSN): user and system. User ones can only be seen and used by the current Windows user, whereas system ones can be seen and used by any Windows user on that same PC.

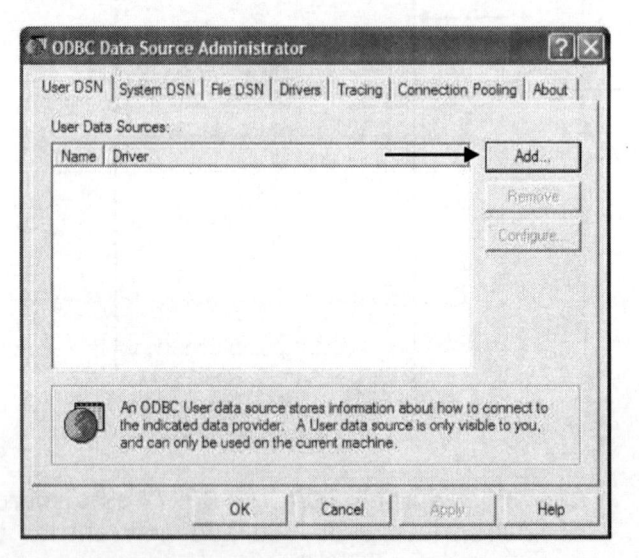

Figure 7: ODBC Admin Main Screen

Introduction to Oracle

When you pres the "*Add*" button, you will see the data set definition wizard's first page as shown here in Figure 8 – where you are to pick the lower layer, database vendor specific ODBC driver (refer back to Figure 5). Here we had the choice between the Microsoft generic Oracle driver and the Oracle 10g one. Generally speaking you will have the most reliable results and fastest performance using the ODBC driver from the database vendor.

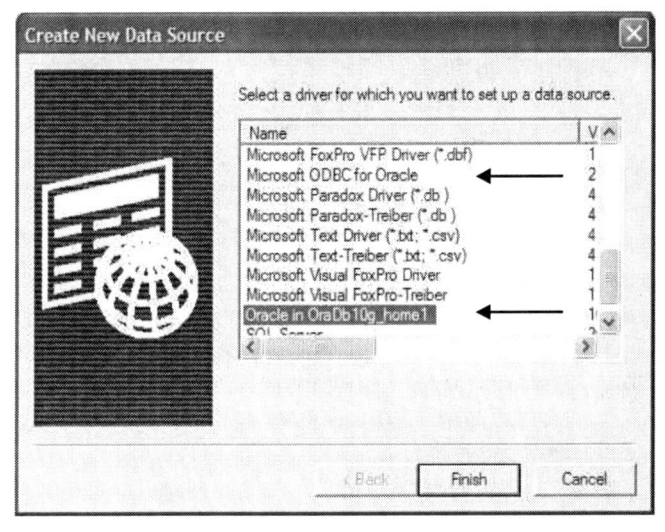

Figure 8: ODBC Driver Selection

Once you've chosen your ODBC driver, you then need to assign some properties to this new data source as shown here in Figure 9 – with the two most important being the data source name (i.e. what will display in the

Connecting   **35**

drop-down list back in Figure 6) and the target database name or service.

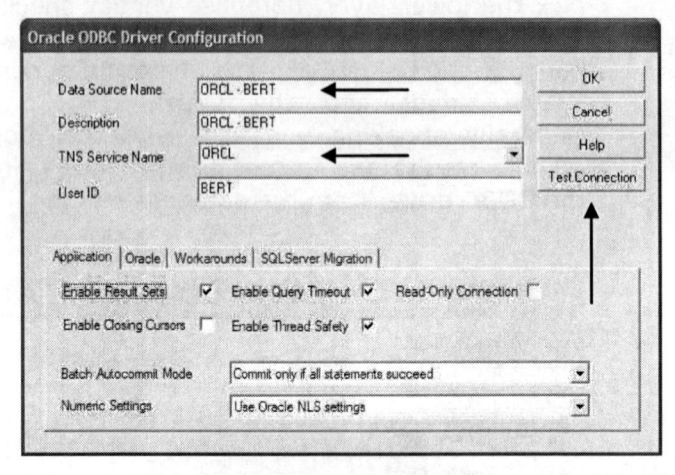

Figure 9: ODBC Configuration

You should of course verify your new data source's correctness by pressing the *"Test Connection"* button. Once it returns *"successful"* you have created a valid ODBC data source.

JDBC Connections

In many respects JDBC is much like ODBC, however it's based on the JAVA language and standard rather than on the Windows applications standard. But it works on Windows, so you may in fact need to use it.

Introduction to Oracle

Note that JDBC offers three types of connections: thick, thin and ODBC bridge. Basically when you choose the thick option you are simply asking JDBC to directly call the Oracle SQL*Net client or OCI layer just like ODBC does. When you choose the bridge option then JDBC simply calls ODBC and your ODBC data sources. Thus you merely have to choose that method and name the data source as shown here in Figure 10. But you now have two layers of code to get to OCI.

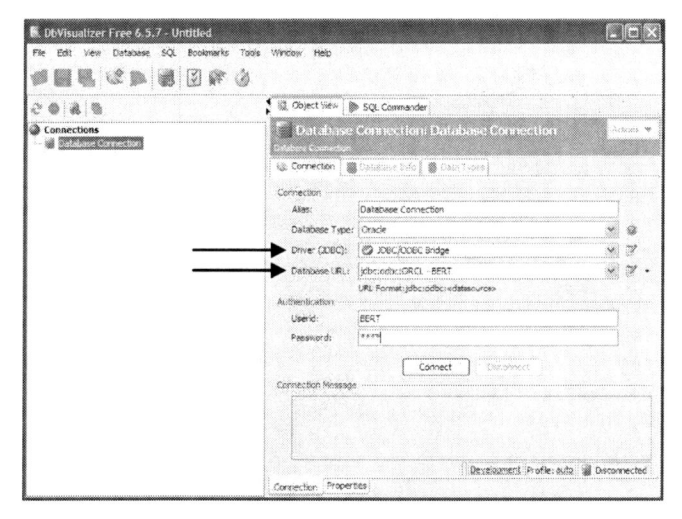

Figure 10: JDBC/ODBC Bridge Connection

The JAVA based database tool shown above in Figure 9 is called DbVisualizer (http://www.dbvis.com). It runs on most desktop operating systems (e.g. Windows,

Linux, MacOS, etc.) and can also connect to almost any database platform.

When you choose the thin JDBC connection option you have to handle something new and different – namely the URL to access the database. Since JDBC does not use the TNANAMES.ora file nor its aliases, you have to enter that information as part of the connect sting as shown here in Figure 11.

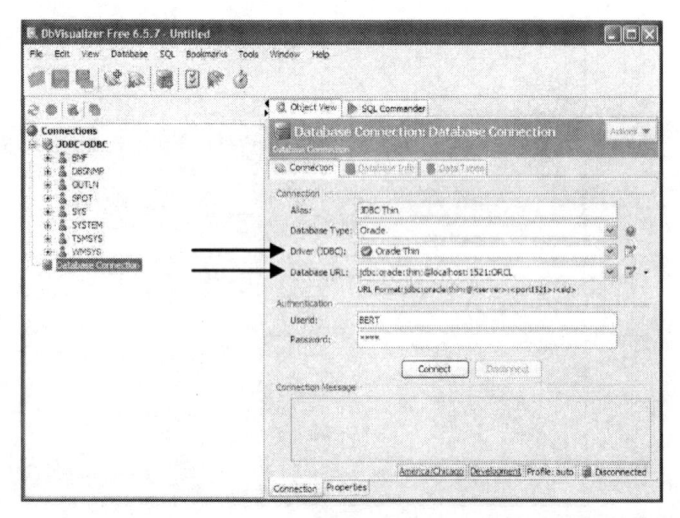

Figure 11: JDBC Thin Connection

The database URL is generally the prefix "jdbc:oracle:thin" followed by the TNS alias type information of the form "IP Address or hosts_alias:port (default=1521):database name. In my case localhost equates to

38   Introduction to Oracle

127.0.0.1, which means the database is running locally on my PC.

Conclusion

In this chapter we reviewed used our basic terminology and prerequisites knowledge to tackle the first and most critical database task – connecting. Much like a phone call – we entered the information necessary to dial in to the database and then placed the call. And much like a phone call the connection will persist until we hang up or the operator (i.e. DBA) kills the line. In the DBA's case that could be based on user inactivity for a specified amount of time. Now that you can talk to or connect to the database, it's time to start looking at the SQL language and database tools to actually perform real work with your data.

Chapter 4: Database Objects

Now that you can successfully connect to your Oracle databases, the natural and logical question is "What are you allowed to do?" Your DBA will have assigned your schema or user a set of privileges as to what is permissible. If you have been granted permissions to simply connect to the database and use already existing database objects, then you won't be able to execute many of the object creation commands in this chapter. But you should read this chapter nonetheless to understand what those database objects are.

Data Definition Language

The SQL language has two basic types of commands: those for creating and altering database objects and those for accessing and working with the data in those objects. The CREATE and ALTER commands belong to the first type, and are referred to as DDL for "*Data Definition Language*" statements. The SELECT, INSERT, UPDATE and DELETE belong to the second type, and are known as DML for "*Data Manipulation Language*" statements. In this chapter we'll be covering DDL commands for the basic and most frequently used database objects. Remember, DDL commands require the DBA to have granted you the requisite privileges to perform them.

Note – at the end of this chapter are syntax diagrams for the CREATE and ALTER commands. You may want to bookmark these for future reference.

Tables

The "*table*" is the key database object. Recall from Chapter 1 that relational databases are required by Codd's rules to store data in tables possessing rows and columns. Thus all relational database management systems must offer tables.

A table is nothing more than a persistent database object or container for your structured data. Structured data simply means that the business recognizes and defines the business objects along with their characteristics or properties. In the old days that would have been a file record layout, now it's the table definition. A table should contain the business data the way the business knows it – and not in some information systems person's idea of the best technical way to do it.

You will want to define multiple varied containers for the different business objects that you work with. So if you work with the business concepts of customers and orders, then you might create CUSTOMER and ORDER tables. Their structure will be different because the business assigns the important characteristics or properties that each must have – which become the columns in a table. Figure 1 shows an example of a simple CREATE TABLE command.

```
CREATE TABLE customer (
first_name    VARCHAR(20) NOT NULL,
last_name     VARCHAR(30) NOT NULL,
phone_num     VARCHAR(10),
street_name   VARCHAR(40),
city_name     VARCHAR(20),
state_code    CHAR(2),
zip_code      CHAR(5)
);
```

Figure 1: CREATE TABLE syntax

The CREATE TABLE command syntax is pretty easy, you simply name the table, define the column names, their data types (including length or size) and whether they are optional or mandatory (i.e. NOT NULL). Figure 2 shows this CREATE TABLE command for the CUSTOMER table executed in Oracle's SQL*Plus.

```
Command Prompt - sqlplus BERT/BERT@ORCL

C:\Temp>
C:\Temp>sqlplus BERT/BERT@ORCL

SQL*Plus: Release 10.2.0.4.0 - Production on Sun Jan 10 10:41:01 2010

Copyright (c) 1982, 2007, Oracle.  All Rights Reserved.

Connected to:
Oracle Database 10g Enterprise Edition Release 10.2.0.4.0 - Production
With the Partitioning, OLAP, Data Mining and Real Application Testing options

SQL> CREATE TABLE customer (
  2    first_name   VARCHAR(20) NOT NULL,
  3    last_name    VARCHAR(30) NOT NULL,
  4    phone_num    VARCHAR(10),
  5    street_name  VARCHAR(40),
  6    city_name    VARCHAR(20),
  7    state_code   CHAR(2),
  8    zip_code     CHAR(5)
  9  );

Table created.

SQL>
```

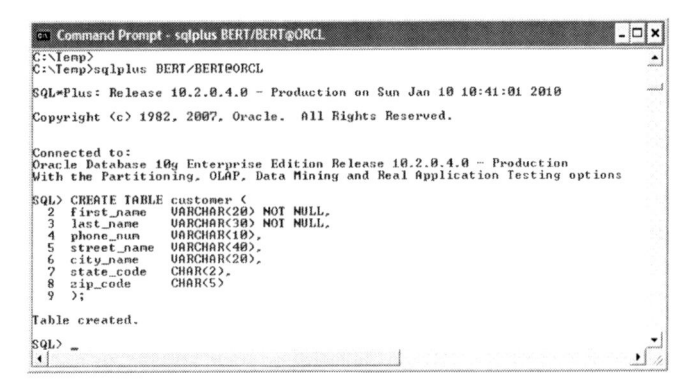

Figure 2: CREATE TABLE executed

Now that you have seen the command syntax and understand what's happening, you would of course instead use a graphical tool like TOAD or SQL Developer to accomplish the task much easier and quicker as shown in here Figure 3.

Database Objects   43

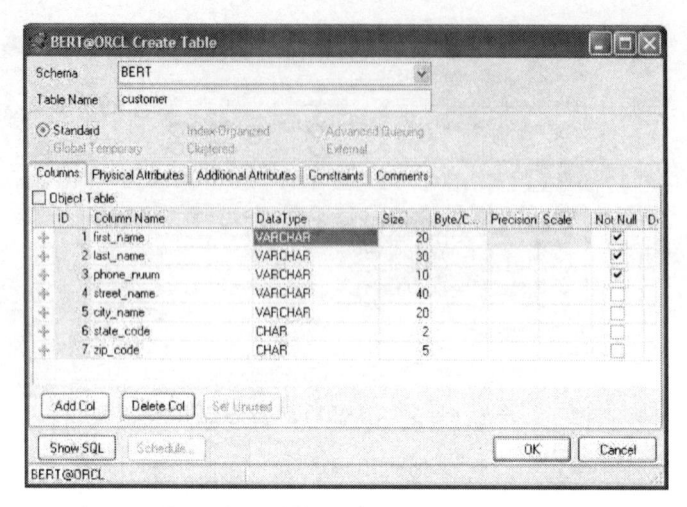

Figure 3: Using GUI rather than syntax

Table 1 contains the names and brief description for the more common data types you are likely to need or work with. There are of course many others, reference the Oracle SQL Reference manual for a complete list.

CHAR(n)	fixed-length character string that blank-pads to the length n=length
VARCHAR(n)	variable-length character string (no blank padding) n=length
NUMBER(p,s)	positive & negative numbers with absolute values between 1.0×10^{-130} and 1.0×10^{126} p= total number of decimal digits s= number of digits to the right of the decimal point
INTEGER	Shorthand for NUMBER(38)
DATE	date and time information: century, year, month, date, hour, minute, and second
TIMESTAMP(p)	extension of DATE data type for storing very precise time values p=fractional seconds precision
BLOB	unstructured binary large objects such as images
CLOB	extremely large character data type for massive text

Table 1: Common Data Types

Key Constraints

The next optional step you may perform when creating a table is to define primary and/or unique key constraints. Note too that you can also embed such constraint definitions in the CREATE TABLE statement itself such that they exist from creation time forward – so that no one inserts an data before the constraints are in place. Refer back to Chapter 1 for a description of the differences between key constraints and indexes – one implements a business rule and the other is a database mechanism for quick access.

So let's say the business tells you that no two customers can have the same first name, last name and phone number. Thus every customer can be uniquely recognized and indentified by the combination of these three pieces of information. To effect that change you would have to alter the table – and you'd have to make two changes.

Since no part of a primary or unique key can be optional, first you must make the phone number a required column. And second, you need to define the primary key constraint on the concatenation of those three columns. Figure 4 shows the ALTER TABLE commands that are required.

```
ALTER TABLE customer
   MODIFY (phone_num NOT NULL);

ALTER TABLE customer
   ADD (PRIMARY KEY
      (first_name, last_name, phone_num));
```

Figure 4: ALTER TABLE syntax

Indexes

The next and final optional step you may perform when creating a table is to define indexes. Maybe either the business tells you or just know from experience that users will often search this table on the state code – and they want fast access based on it. Thus you will need to create an index on that table and column as shown here in Figure 5.

```
CREATE INDEX cust_index2
   ON customer (phone_num);
```

Figure 5: CREATE INDEX syntax

So why was this index named as the second customer index? Because we know that key constraints are implemented via indexes and the prior primary key constraint created the first index on this table. So as shown in Figure 6, TOAD shows that the table has two indexes: one with three columns for the

Database Objects

constraint that the system named for us, and the named one specifically created.

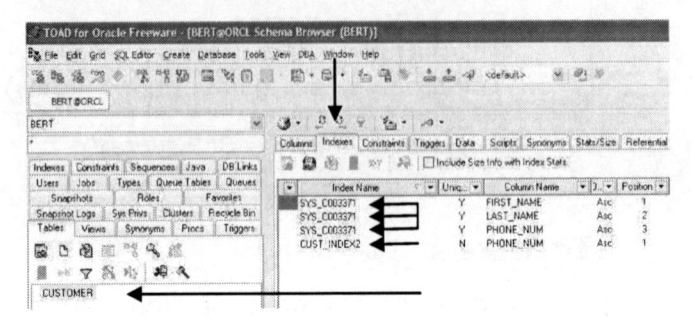

Figure 6: Indexes on Table

Views

A view is nothing more than a subset of or *"picture window"* into one or more tables' columns. If the employee table has a salary column, that might be considered sensitive or privileged data. Thus managers might be able to access the table and all its columns, but employees are only supposed to see the columns minus salary. For that we can create a view as shown in Figure 7 and have non-managers access employee data via the view. Note that another way to do this would be to use Oracle's built-in security to define grants at the column level.

```
CREATE TABLE employee (
emp_num      INTEGER      NOT NULL,
first_name   VARCHAR(20)  NOT NULL,
last_name    VARCHAR(30)  NOT NULL,
salary       NUMBER(8,2)  NOT NULL,
phone_num    VARCHAR(10),
street_name  VARCHAR(40),
city_name    VARCHAR(20),
state_code   CHAR(2),
zip_code     CHAR(5)
);

CREATE VIEW emp_view AS
SELECT emp_num, first_name,
last_name, phone_num,
       street_name, city_name,
state_code, zip_code
FROM employee;
```

Figure 7: CREATE VIEW syntax

The SELECT command is something new and covered more thoroughly in a later chapter. For now, this SELECT is simply informing Oracle that when you work with the EMP_VIEW view that you are limited to seeing all the EMPLOYEE table columns but salary.

There is another reason why views are so useful (besides the security aspect). What if the business defines a query or report and wants to make sure that all database users always enter the correct command syntax. For example if the employee name must always show up on reports and screens as last name, comma, first name – then a view such as the one in Figure 8 can address that need.

```
CREATE VIEW emp_view2 (
emp_num, full_name, phone_num,
street_name, city_name, state_code,
zip_code
)
AS
SELECT emp_num,
last_name||','||first_name,
phone_num, street_name, city_name,
state_code, zip_code
FROM employee;
```

Figure 8: Complex View syntax

This view command is a little more complex. Since we want to essentially create a new, virtual column on the fly, we have to name the columns as if we're doing a create table command. That's where **full_name** comes from. Then we have to tell the database what columns we want as with any view, plus we have to instruct Oracle on how to construct that virtual column. That's where the expression **last_name||','||first_name** comes from. The two new syntax items here are the concatenation operator || and a literal string, which are characters enclosed in quotes.

Finally an advanced and very powerful use for views is creating a single view definition that

50 Introduction to Oracle

"*glues together*" or "*joins*" multiple related tables (refer to Chapter 6 for more about joins). Thus if users always need to query multiple tables together to correctly see the whole and true "*business picture*", then one can create a view to make those multiple tables appear as one. In other words it lets one hide the physical table design from the business reality.

Conclusion

In this chapter learned what the basic database objects are plus some of their CREATE AND ALTER commands. These types of commands as generally referred to as DDL for Data Definition Language – and they often require your DBA to have granted you the rights to perform them. While the tables, constraints, indexes and views discussed in this chapter are a tiny subset of the overall database objects offered these days, they are nonetheless the ones used most often. Thus a fundamental knowledge of these base database objects is often sufficient to begin working with your Oracle databases.

Syntax Charts

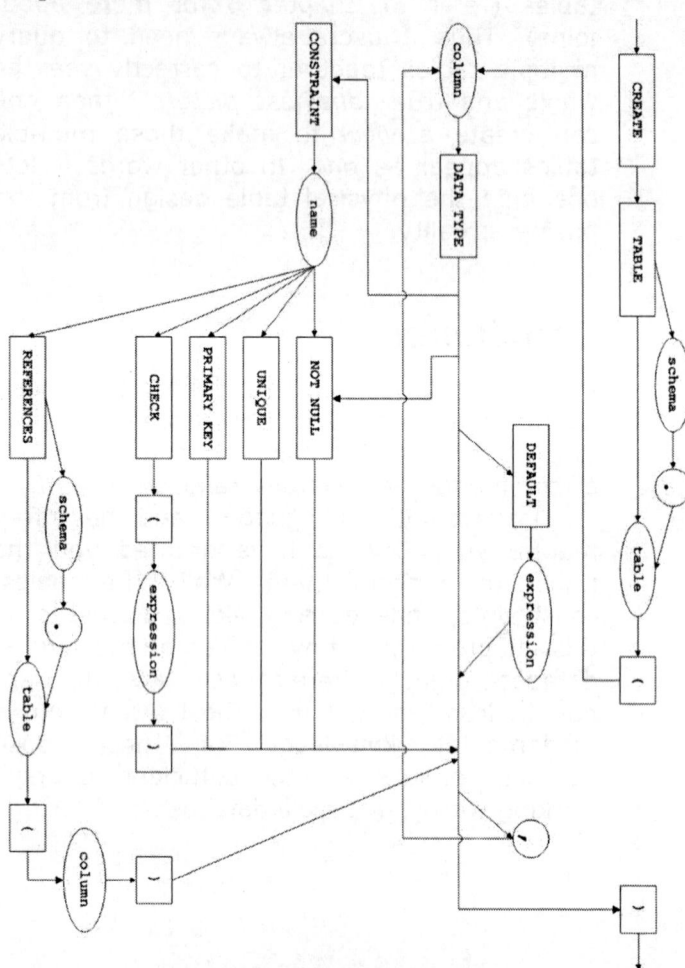

Figure 9: CREATE TABLE

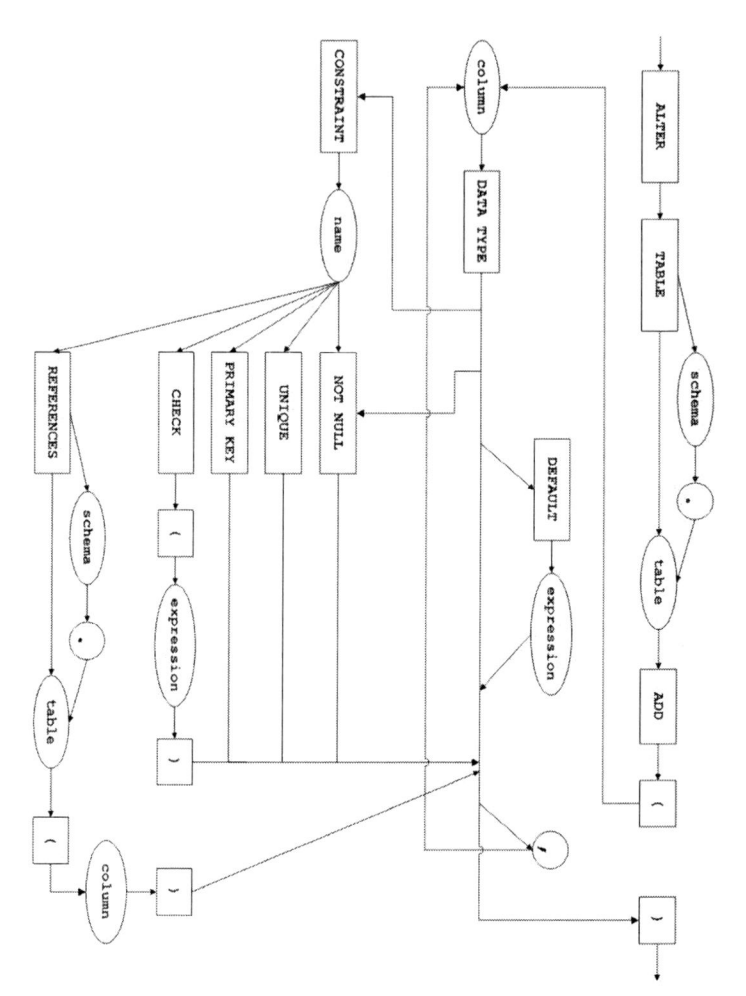

Figure 10: ALTER TABLE - ADD

Database Objects 53

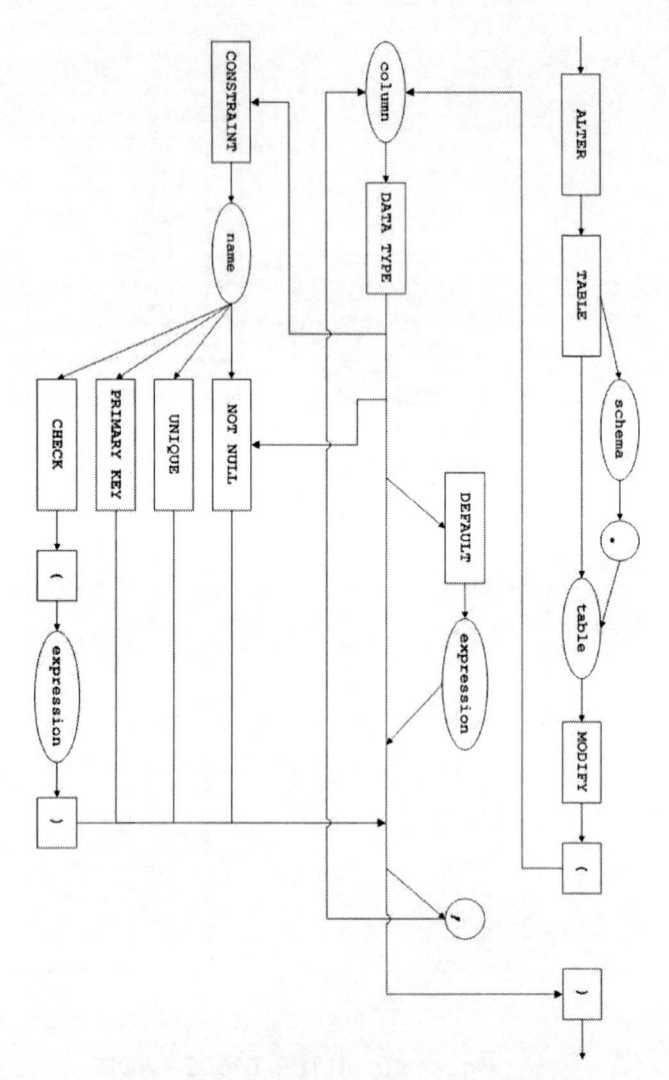

Figure 11: ALTER TABLE - MODIFY

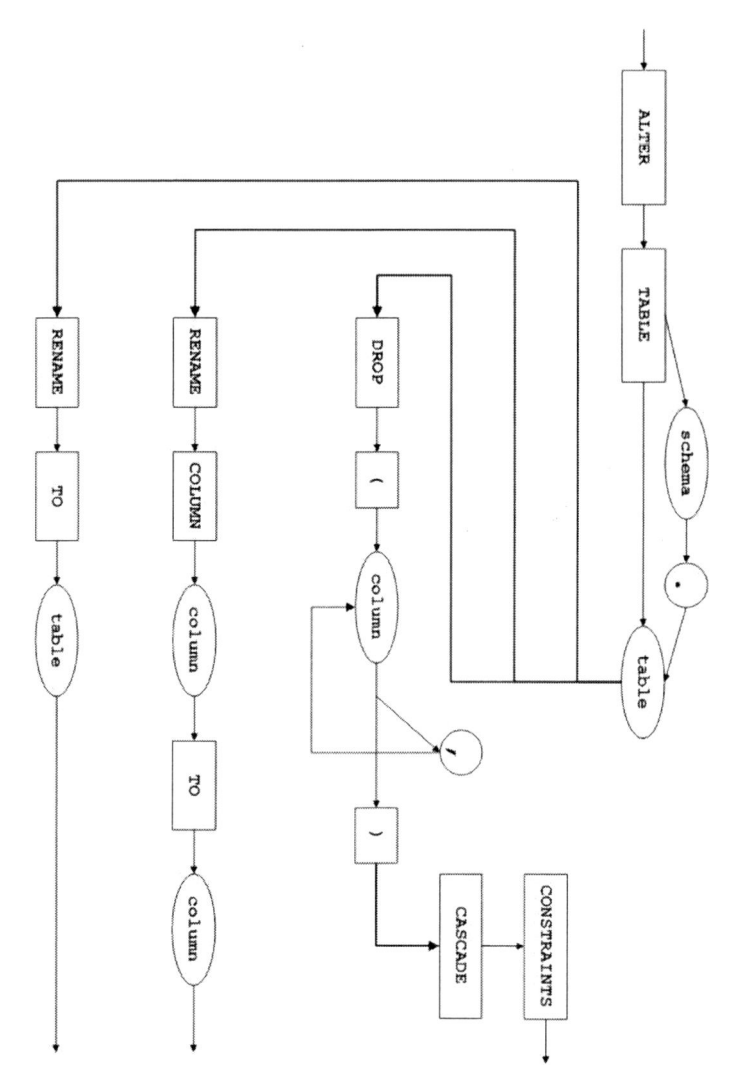

Figure 12: ALTER TABLE - DROP/RENAME

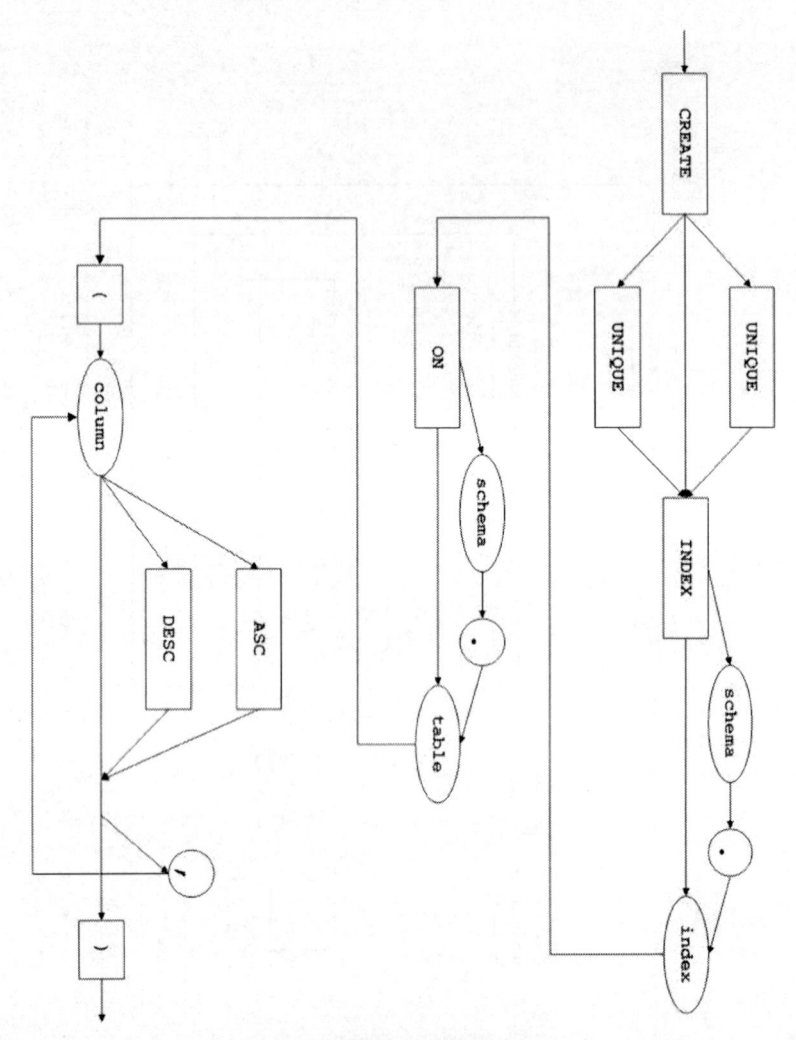

Figure 13: CREATE INDEX

Chapter 5: Basic SQL

The first four chapters have taken you from defining Oracle, to connecting with the database and creating some rudimentary database objects. Thus it's now time to begin learning the SQL or Structured Query Language. There are four Data Manipulation (i.e. DML) commands and two transaction control commands. Even if you will never type these commands per se, you will need to understand their nature. Because even when you use a graphical tool like TOAD, SQL Developer, Excel or Access, the actions that you'll be performing graphically will be based upon these basic SQL commands.

COMMIT

The first transactional command is COMMIT, which allows one to past changes to the database. The syntax is as follows:

COMMIT { WORK }

Where the word WORK is optional, but permitted so as to adhere to the ANSI SQL standard.

When you connect to the database you have begun a session. Any work which you perform during that session can only be seen by you until you instruct the database to *"make it so"*. That is accomplished via the COMMIT command. Since we've not yet gone over the DML commands, let's for now look at an example using a graphical user interface tool like TOAD as shown here in Figure 1.

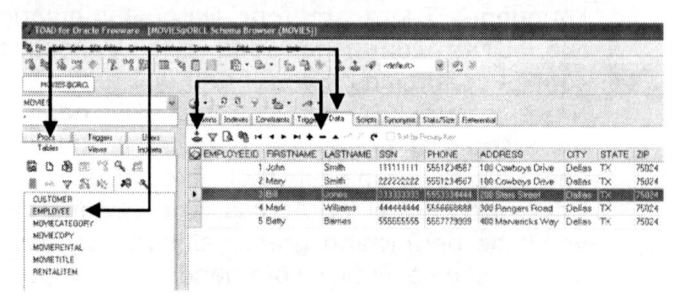

Figure 1: DELETE & COMMIT a Row

The outer arrows show that the focus is on tables and their data, plus that the EMPLOYEE table was chosen. The inner arrows point to the toolbar icons for DELETE record (i.e. minus sign) and COMMIT (i.e. arrow pointing into a disk). The table's data appears as rows and columns, much like a spreadsheet. Finally the row or record for employee *"Bill Jones"* has been highlighted.

To delete the selected row or record, you would simply press the toolbar icon for

DELETE record (i.e. minus sign). But that change would not yet be real. That is other people querying the same table would still see the record for "*Bill Jones*". It would not yet have been really deleted. But then once you press the toolbar icon to COMMIT (i.e. arrow pointing into a disk), now the database makes any and all of your session's changes to that table permanent – and thus their effects become visible to all users.

ROLLBACK

The second transactional command is ROLLBACK. The syntax is as follows:

ROLLBACK { WORK }

Where the word WORK is optional, but permitted so as to adhere to the ANSI SQL standard.

ROLLBACK is pretty much just the opposite of a COMMIT, which is that all of a session's interim work is simply undone or thrown away. Since the actions were never committed to the database, no one has ever seen the end results. Think of it as the "*I've changed my mind*" command.

Using the spreadsheet analogy, assume that you open a spreadsheet file and make changes. If another user now opens that file they do not see your changes. If you "save" the file and now the second person opens it, your changes would now be visible or committed. If you instead had closed Excel and chosen not to save your work, now the spreadsheet file is back to the exact same state as when you opened it – or rolled back.

INSERT

The first DML command is INSERT, which allows one to create or add new rows to a table. The basic syntax is:

> INSERT INTO table_name VALUES (value_1 {, value_2, value_3, ... })

There generally will be one value listed per column in the table. Thus you need to know what the table looks like or its structure in order to know the number and kind of values to enter. Figure 2 shows a CREATE TABLE statement followed by five INSERT command examples for that table.

```
CREATE TABLE people (
  rec_no   INTEGER      NOT NULL,
  name     VARCHAR(30)  NOT NULL,
  city     VARCHAR(20),
  state    CHAR(2)
);
INSERT INTO people VALUES (1,
  'John Wayne','Dallas','TX');
INSERT INTO people VALUES (2,
  'Clark Gable','Fort Worth','TX');
INSERT INTO people VALUES (3,
  'Errol Flynn','Austin','TX');
INSERT INTO people VALUES (4,
  'Betty Davis', NULL, NULL);
INSERT INTO people VALUES (5,
  'Gina Davis');
```

Figure 2: INSERT Examples

The first three INSERT examples in Figure 2 look pretty much as expected. Note though that the fourth INSERT uses the special NULL keyword – which means empty or no value. Since the city and state columns were defined as being optional, you do not have to provide a real value for them to the INSERT command. But look at the fifth INSERT which tries to entirely skip providing those two values. The database will report the *"not enough values"* error. So the NULL keyword serves as the placeholder to tell the database no value, and it has to be there even for an optional column.

Basic SQL

Finally, remember that those five INSERT commands would not take effect for others to see unless followed by a COMMIT;

DELETE

The second DML command is DELETE, which allows one to drop existing rows from a table. The basic syntax is:

> DELETE FROM table_name
> { WHERE condition(s) }

Note that the WHERE clause portion of the command is optional. But be careful, as a DELETE command without the WHERE condition will drop every row from the table – making it empty. So in most cases you should include some kind of WHERE conditions. Figure 3 shows a few examples:

```
DELETE FROM people
   WHERE rec_no = 1;
DELETE FROM people
   WHERE state = 'TX';
DELETE FROM people
   WHERE city IS NULL;
DELETE from people
   WHERE city = 'Dallas' OR
         City = 'Fort Worth';
DELETE FROM people
   WHERE name LIKE '%n%';
```

Figure 3: DELETE Examples

Using the four rows that were inserted previously in Figure 2, the five DELETE commands in Figure 3 would behave individually as follows:

- Delete's one record: John Wayne
- Deletes three records: everyone except Betty Davis (remember that Gina Davis was not inserted due to "*not enough values*" error)
- Deletes one record: Betty Davis
- Deletes two records: John Wayne and Clark Gable
- Deletes two records: John Wayne and Eroll Flynn

Basic SQL

Note the special syntax of the last three DELETE examples' WHERE clauses. Let's examine them closer and understand these special WHERE clause syntaxes.

In the third DELETE example, when you want to specify to the database an empty value as part of the WHERE clause there are two requirements. First, as with the INSERT command, you need to use the special NULL keyword. Second and most critical, when using NULL in a WHERE clause you must use specify "IS NULL" or "IS NOT NULL". The equal sign will not function as expected with NULL values. Had you said WHERE city = NULL, the database would return zero rows.

In the fourth DELETE example, note that you can write multiple conditions that must be met and connect them with the conditional operators of "AND" and "OR". Furthermore just as you might write a more complex mathematical expression, you can include parenthesis to clarify and control the conditions' order of precedence. In fact for readability for the next person who may have to look at your SQL, it's advisable to generally include parenthesis.

In the fifth DELETE example, note the new operator "LIKE" and the special meta character "%". LIKE equates to the concept of contains, so in this case the person's name has an "n" in it. Plus that "n" can be anywhere in the string as indicated by the "%", which is simply the wildcard character. Most people are probably more familiar with the asterisk or "*" being the wildcard, but in Oracle it's the percent sign. If we had instead wanted to delete people whose name begin with "J" then the syntax would have been WHERE name LIKE 'J%'.

Finally note that using LIKE is more efficient than the alternative of looking for a substring. Thus the syntax WHERE name like 'J%' is generally superior to the alternative of using expressions containing functions such as WHERE substr(name,1,1) = 'J'. The key difference is that the LIKE syntax will be able to use any underlying index on the name column to speed up access and the substring version will not. On a big table this can make the difference between very fast (i.e. seconds) to unbearable (i.e. minutes or even hours).

UPDATE

The third DML command is UPDATE, which allows one to modify column values for existing rows in a table. The basic syntax is:

    UPDATE FROM table_name
      SET column_1 = value_1,
      {, column_2 = value_2, ... }
      { WHERE condition(s) }

Note that the WHERE clause portion of the command is optional. But be careful, as an UPDATE command without the WHERE condition will modify every row in the table – thus performing a global change. So in most cases you should include some kind of WHERE conditions. Figure 4 shows a few examples:

```
UPDATE people
   SET city = 'Houston'
   WHERE rec_no = 1;
UPDATE people
   SET city = 'Atlanta',
       state = 'GA'
   WHERE state = 'TX';
UPDATE people
   SET city = 'Tampa',
       state = 'FL'
   WHERE city IS NULL;
UPDATE people
   SET city = 'Phoenix',
       State = 'AZ'
   WHERE city = 'Dallas' OR
         City = 'Fort Worth';
UPDATE people
   SET city = 'El Paso'
   WHERE name LIKE '%n%';
```

Figure 4: UPDATE Examples

Using the four rows that were inserted previously in Figure 2, the five UPDATE commands in Figure 4 would behave individually as follows:

- Updates one record: relocated to John Wayne to Houston
- Updates three records: everyone except Betty Davis relocated to Atlanta (remember that Gina Davis was not inserted due to "*not enough values*" error)
- Updates one record: Betty Davis relocated to Tampa
- Updates two records: John Wayne and Clark Gable relocated to Phoenix
- Updates two records: John Wayne and Eroll Flynn relocted to El Paso

Note the special syntax of the last three UPDATE examples' WHERE clauses. They function identically as was described in the prior section for the DELETE command. Refer back to that section for a better description.

SELECT

The fourth and final DML command is SELECT, which allows one to retrieve and display existing rows from a table. The basic syntax is:

>SELECT
>
>   * | column_1 { , column_2 ... }
>
>FROM table_name
>
>{ WHERE condition(s) }

Note that the WHERE clause portion of the command is optional. But be careful, as a SELECT command without the WHERE condition will return every row in the table – so all ten billion rows from a huge table. Since that data has to traverse the network to get to you, you'll tax the network. And in some cases your software and/or PC may not be able to handle the return of that much data – either crashing and/or returning *"insufficient or out of memory"* errors. So in most cases you should include some kind of WHERE conditions.

We're going to incrementally develop SELECT command examples because SELECT is the single most frequently used SQL command. Figure 5 shows the most basic form: SELECT *

FROM table_name, which simply retrieves all the columns (i.e. *) and all the rows (i.e. no WHERE clause) for the table.

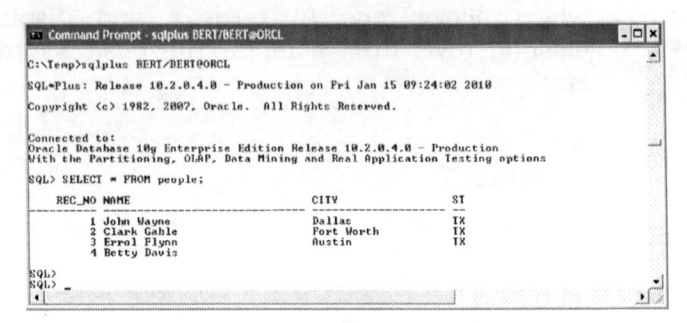

```
Command Prompt - sqlplus BERT/BERT@ORCL
C:\Temp>sqlplus BERT/BERT@ORCL
SQL*Plus: Release 10.2.0.4.0 - Production on Fri Jan 15 09:24:02 2010
Copyright (c) 1982, 2007, Oracle.  All Rights Reserved.

Connected to:
Oracle Database 10g Enterprise Edition Release 10.2.0.4.0 - Production
With the Partitioning, OLAP, Data Mining and Real Application Testing options

SQL> SELECT * FROM people;
    REC_NO NAME                CITY               ST
---------- ------------------- ------------------ ---
         1 John Wayne          Dallas             TX
         2 Clark Gable         Fort Worth         TX
         3 Errol Flynn         Austin             TX
         4 Betty Davis

SQL>
SQL>
```

Figure 5: Simplest SELECT Example

One of the strengths of relational databases is that they are built upon a mathematical foundation, known as relational algebra and relational calculus. Hence everything can be expressed mathematically – and thus one can construct mathematical proofs as to the commands accuracy. We won't go into that other than to say that the relational terms for the SELECT command fall into two categories: projection and restriction.

Projection simply means what columns does the SELECT command display as per the second line of the syntax (i.e. * | column_1 { , column_2 ... }). Thus the asterisk (i.e. *) means project or display all the columns, whereas naming the columns yourself means to project or display just those. Think of projection as what columns of data for from table do I need back from the database in order to accomplish the task at hand. Returning to our spreadsheet analogy, if you cut and paste a range of columns from one worksheet to another then you've performed a "*projection*".

Restriction simply means what rows does the SELECT command display as per the fourth line of the syntax (i.e. WHERE clause). Thus no WHERE clause means no restriction or display all the rows, whereas specifying a WHERE clause means to restrict display just the rows that meet the criteria. Think of restriction as what rows of data for from table do I need back from the database in order to accomplish the task at hand. Returning to our spreadsheet analogy, if you cut and paste a range of rows from one worksheet to another then you've performed a "*restriction*".

Figure 6 shows a more complex and complete SELECT command using all the things we've learned so far.

```
SELECT
   name, city, state
FROM people
WHERE city = 'Dallas' OR
      State = 'TX';
```

Figure 6: Complete SELECT Example

This SELECT example performs both user specified projections and restrictions. Thus this example is much more like the command that you'll be writing. The results for this SELECT are shown here in Figure 7.

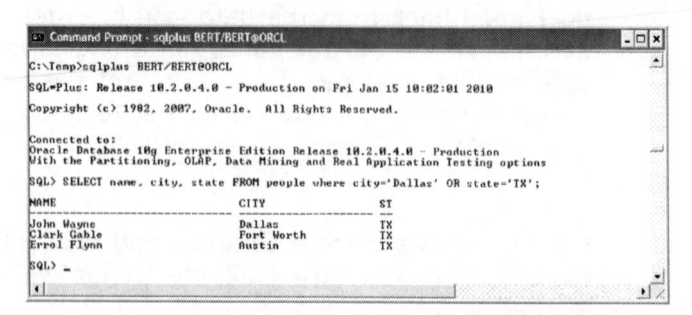

```
Command Prompt - sqlplus BERT/BERT@ORCL

C:\Temp>sqlplus BERT/BERT@ORCL
SQL*Plus: Release 10.2.0.4.0 - Production on Fri Jan 15 10:02:01 2010
Copyright (c) 1982, 2007, Oracle.  All Rights Reserved.

Connected to:
Oracle Database 10g Enterprise Edition Release 10.2.0.4.0 - Production
With the Partitioning, OLAP, Data Mining and Real Application Testing options

SQL> SELECT name, city, state FROM people where city='Dallas' OR state='TX';

NAME                          CITY                  ST
----------------------------  --------------------  --
John Wayne                    Dallas                TX
Clark Gable                   Fort Worth            TX
Errol Flynn                   Austin                TX

SQL>
```

Figure 7: Complete SELECT Output

While SELECT is the most frequently used SQL command, it's also is the most complex. However in this chapter we learned just the very basics. The SELECT command will be covered more thoroughly in the chapter for Advanced SQL. What we've covered in this

72 Introduction to Oracle

chapter is probably 10% of what the SELECT command syntax has to offer.

Conclusion

In this chapter we covered the most basic SQL commands and their syntax. We've built upon all that we've learned so far to actually INSERT, DELETE, UPDATE and SELECT data from tables. Plus we learned how to make any data changes permanent (i.e. COMMIT) or to be undone (i.e. ROLLBACK). With just these basics you now have a fundamental working knowledge of the SQL language, and thus how to work with your databases. It would be worth stopping here and *"test driving"* what you now know on your database before proceeding. Because next we're going to take this knowledge to the next level – and that's about ten times more complex than this material. Some experience is thus advisable.

Chapter 6: Advanced SQL

The last chapter went over the six basic SQL commands that you'll use most often – but just in their simplest forms. Now we'll incrementally delve into more complex versions of the SELECT command and thereby answer more complex business questions. Again you may not end up writing such SELECT commands, but rather using some graphical tool to communicate your desires and having it generate the SQL. But you'll need to understand this chapter's concepts in order to comprehend and therefore utilize those graphical representations.

NOTE: This chapter's sections and examples are each added to the basic SELECT syntax to keep things easy. At the end there are examples showing how all these individual constructs can be utilized together to form highly complex SELECT statements.

ORDER BY

When you SELECT data from a table, the database engine is free to return the records or rows in whatever manner is most expedient – often in an order that has nothing to do with any business criteria. Thus if you want the rows returned sorted by some meaningful business characteristics, you must instruct the database to sort the rows before returning them to you. For that the basic SELECT syntax is expanded upon as follows (with the new clause indicated in bold).

SELECT
   * | column_1 { , column_2 ... }
FROM table_name
{ WHERE condition(s) }
{ ORDER BY
   column_1 {ASC|DESC}
{ ,column_2 {ASC|DESC}... }}

Note that you can sort by one or more columns and optionally in ascending or descending order per column, with ascending being the default. Figure 1 shows an example of sorting by the city column of the people table developed in the last chapter.

Advanced SQL   **75**

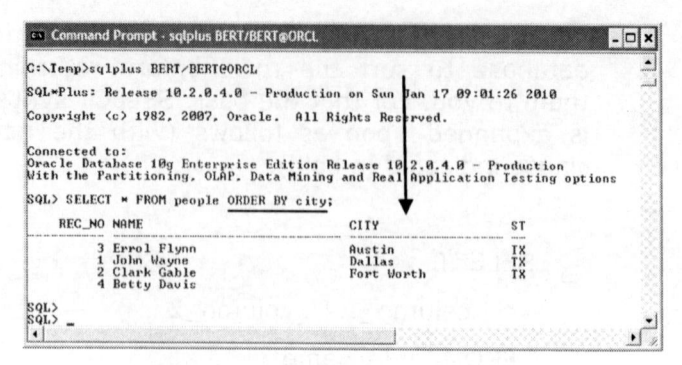

```
C:\Temp>sqlplus BERT/BERT@ORCL

SQL*Plus: Release 10.2.0.4.0 - Production on Sun Jan 17 09:01:26 2010
Copyright (c) 1982, 2007, Oracle.  All Rights Reserved.

Connected to:
Oracle Database 10g Enterprise Edition Release 10.2.0.4.0 - Production
With the Partitioning, OLAP, Data Mining and Real Application Testing options

SQL> SELECT * FROM people ORDER BY city;

    REC_NO NAME                    CITY                 ST
---------- ----------------------- -------------------- ----
         3 Errol Flynn             Austin               TX
         1 John Wayne              Dallas               TX
         2 Clark Gable             Fort Worth           TX
         4 Betty Davis

SQL>
SQL>
```

Figure 1: ORDER BY Example

The ORDER BY clause introduces a measurable performance penalty as the database engine must first gather all the desired rows, then sort and return them. Of course the more data expected to be returned the larger the performance penalty. But if you need the data in a guaranteed order, you must add the ORDER BY clause.

Note: Sometimes the database will by sheer luck seemingly return the rows in sorted order. But only utilizing the ORDER BY clause can guarantee this.

GROUP BY

Sometimes the business question at hand requires one row of output for each grouping of similar rows. For example you might want to know how many people live in each state.

But if you just try a GROUP BY with a simple SELECT * you'll get the "*not a group by expression*" error shown here in Figure 2.

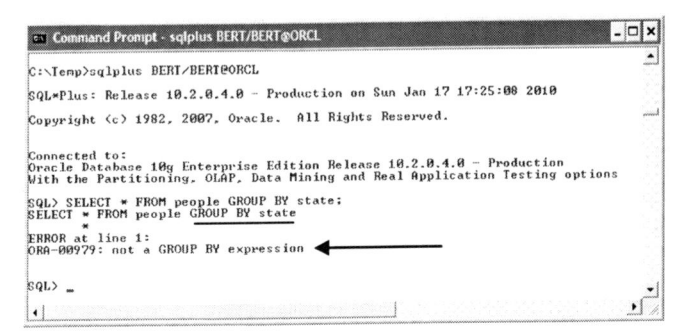

Figure 2: GROUP BY Error

Whenever you use a GROUP BY clause there are generally three additional requirements: the projection criteria must include a "*group*" function, the GROUP BY clause must specify the columns construct groupings for, and often the projection criteria will also include the same columns as the GROUP BY clause – that way you have a meaningful column of data to go with each of the group function row results. Figure 3 shows the correct syntax for querying how many people live in each state.

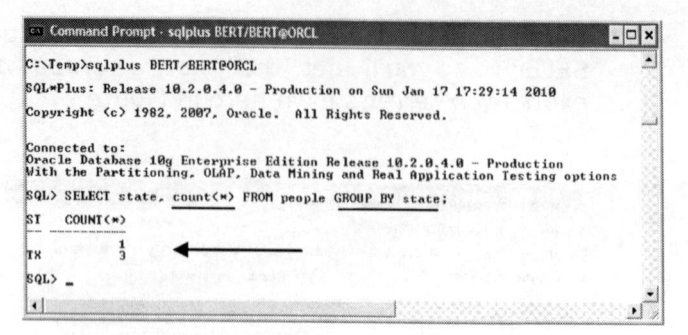

Figure 3: GROUP BY Row Example

Note the first row of output – there's one person whose state is NULL. The second rows shows that there are 3 people whose state is Texas. When constructing typical business queries and reports, you'll use the GROUP BY syntax often. It's a very powerful tool.

So what are these "*group*" functions? They are functions returning one value when applied to the columns specified for that grouping. The asterisk (i.e. *) simply means to use the entire record as the grouping column. In Figure 3 the COUNT(*) grouping function was used to simply count how many rows of people occur per unique state value. In many cases you'll specify a column like shown here in Figure 4.

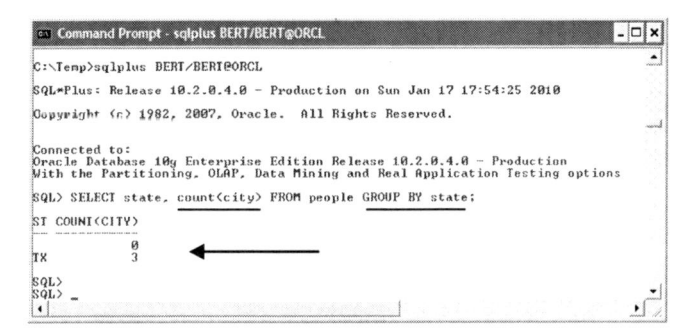

```
Command Prompt - sqlplus BERT/BERT@ORCL

C:\Temp>sqlplus BERT/BERT@ORCL
SQL*Plus: Release 10.2.0.4.0 - Production on Sun Jan 17 17:54:25 2010
Copyright (c) 1982, 2007, Oracle.  All Rights Reserved.

Connected to:
Oracle Database 10g Enterprise Edition Release 10.2.0.4.0 - Production
With the Partitioning, OLAP, Data Mining and Real Application Testing options

SQL> SELECT state, count(city) FROM people GROUP BY state;

ST COUNT(CITY)
-- -----------
             0
TX           3

SQL>
SQL>
```

Figure 4: GROUP BY Column Example

There are many group functions, but the ones you'll at first and most often include:

- AVG
- COUNT
- MAX
- MEDIAN
- MIN
- STDDEV
- SUM

Did you notice the seemingly odd difference for the NULL records between Figure 3 and Figure 4? Figure 3 shows one record for the NULL state, but Figure 4 shows zero. Why are they different? Remember that you must use IS NULL and IS NOT NULL in WHERE clauses because NULL's do not behave the way you might expect. The same is true when you apply any function to a NULL value – the result is always zero!

HAVING

The HAVING clause is actually very simple in concept, but it's quite often considered one of the seemingly more confusing features. The WHERE clause performs restrictions at the row level and thus eliminates table rows from being included. Whereas the HAVING clause performs restrictions at the group level and thus eliminates group function resulting rows from being included. So the WHERE clause occurs before the group function whereas the HAVING clause occurs after. Knowing this simple fact alone can often help you to decide when to use one clause versus the other.

So how can we modify the query in Figure 4 to only include those results where the city count is greater than zero and thus eliminate that first, kind of meaningless row? That's exactly what the HAVING clause is for, and the syntax would be like that shown in Figure 5.

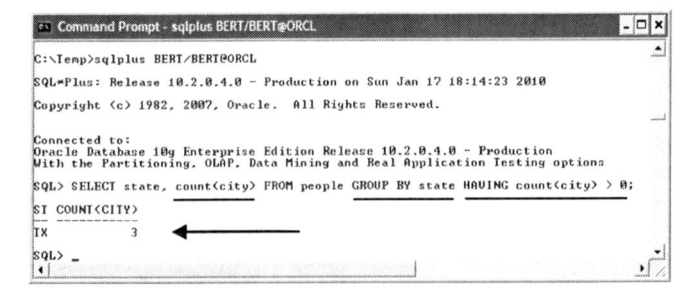

Figure 5: HAVING Example

Finally note that while the GROUP BY creates groupings, it doesn't sort their output order. So if multiple grouping rows are to be returned and you want them sorted, you must also use the ORDER BY clause. A common mistake is to assume that the GROUP BY clause somehow does both and to leave the ORDER BY clause off.

DISTINCT

Sometimes you may need to know what the range or universe of existing values are for a column. For example we may want to know what cities exist within the people table. For that we need to use the DISTINCT clause as shown here in Figure 6.

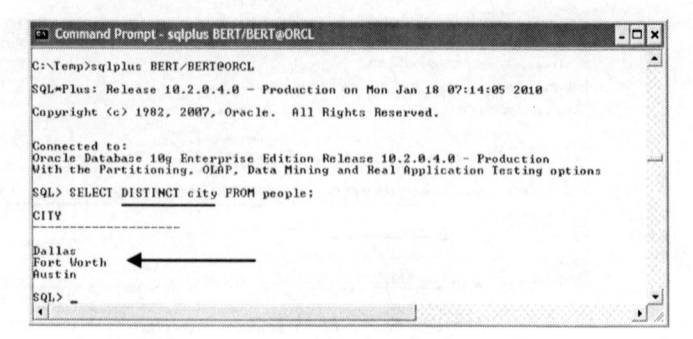

```
Command Prompt - sqlplus BERT/BERT@ORCL

C:\Temp>sqlplus BERT/BERT@ORCL
SQL*Plus: Release 10.2.0.4.0 - Production on Mon Jan 18 07:14:05 2010
Copyright (c) 1982, 2007, Oracle.  All Rights Reserved.

Connected to:
Oracle Database 10g Enterprise Edition Release 10.2.0.4.0 - Production
With the Partitioning, OLAP, Data Mining and Real Application Testing options

SQL> SELECT DISTINCT city FROM people;

CITY
--------------------
Dallas
Fort Worth      ←
Austin

SQL>
```

Figure 6: DISTINCT Example

The DISTINCT clause introduces a measurable performance penalty as the database engine must first gather all the desired rows, sort them and then return one value per group. Of course the more data expected to be returned the larger the performance penalty. But if you need to know the list of unique values for a column, then consider utilizing the DISTINCT clause.

However always make sure that your need is genuine and that DISTINCT is the only or best way to solve the problem. Because the DISTINCT clause is probably the most overused SELECT construct – very often used as a crutch when the problem and the efficient SQL for it are a little less obvious. In these cases people will often fall back or resort to use the DISTINCT clause to quickly (but very inefficiently) dig them out of a SQL coding quandary.

JOINS

Thus far all the SELECT examples have operated upon a single table, hence the FROM clauses have each listed just one table. However optimal relational design often adheres to the principles of *"data normalization"*, which simply means to break the data up into more smaller but related tables to reduce data redundancy – which should then translate into more accurate data. But it's not uncommon for those more familiar with *"flat file"* record design to construct a single large table like the one shown here in Figure 7.

```
CREATE TABLE BIG_EMP (
EMPNO      NUMBER(4)       NOT NULL,
ENAME      VARCHAR2(10)    NOT NULL,
JOB        VARCHAR2(9)     NOT NULL,
MGR        NUMBER(4),
HIREDATE   DATE            NOT NULL,
SAL        NUMBER(7,2)     NOT NULL,
COMM       NUMBER(7,2),
DEPTNO     NUMBER(2)       NOT NULL,
DNAME      VARCHAR2(14)    NOT NULL,
LOC        VARCHAR2(13)    NOT NULL
);
```

Figure 7: Poor Table Design

Which results in data like shown here in Figure 8.

EMPNO	ENAME	JOB	MGR	HIREDATE	SAL	COMM	DEPTNO	DNAME	LOC
7782	CLARK	MANAGER	7839	6/9/1981	2450		10	ACCOUNTING	NEW YORK
7839	KING	PRESIDENT		11/17/1981	5000		10	ACCOUNTING	NEW YORK
7934	MILLER	CLERK	7782	1/23/1982	1300		10	ACCOUNTING	NEW YORK
7369	SMITH	CLERK	7902	12/17/1980	800		20	RESEARCH	DALLAS
7566	JONES	MANAGER	7839	4/2/1981	2975		20	RESEARCH	DALLAS
7788	SCOTT	ANALYST	7566	12/9/1982	3000		20	RESEARCH	DALLAS
7876	ADAMS	CLERK	7788	1/12/1983	1100		20	RESEARCH	DALLAS
7902	FORD	ANALYST	7566	12/3/1981	3000		20	RESEARCH	DALLAS
7499	ALLEN	SALESMAN	7698	2/20/1981	1600	300	30	SALES	CHICAGO
7521	WARD	SALESMAN	7698	2/22/1981	1250	500	30	SALES	CHICAGO
7654	MARTIN	SALESMAN	7698	9/28/1981	1250	1400	30	SALES	CHICAGO
7698	BLAKE	MANAGER	7839	5/1/1981	2850		30	SALES	CHICAGO
7844	TURNER	SALESMAN	7698	9/8/1981	1500	0	30	SALES	CHICAGO
7900	JAMES	CLERK	7698	12/3/1981	950		30	SALES	CHICAGO

Figure 8: Poor Table Data

There are two problems with this table design and its data. First, the fact that the research department is located in Dallas is repeated once for every employee in that department. Thus to relocate the research department to Houston you'd have to update every employee in that department. So what if the research department had 50,000 employees – that update could take a while. Second, what if the update accidentally missed some of those employee records? Then we'd have a business quandary whereby a single department exists in two locations. It's this second problem that will almost always occur over time, and hence why normalizing table designs is such a critical concept.

Thus the more relationally correct and preferred design would be to split this big table into two smaller related tables as shown here by Figure 9. Since the department number, name and location only depend upon the department number, those columns are split off into a separate table. The department number is then left in the employee table as a logical pointer known as the foreign key (refer back to Chapter 1 for the definition and Chapter 4 for the create table syntax).

```
CREATE TABLE EMP (
EMPNO      NUMBER(4)      NOT NULL,
ENAME      VARCHAR2(10)   NOT NULL,
JOB        VARCHAR2(9)    NOT NULL,
MGR        NUMBER(4),
HIREDATE   DATE           NOT NULL,
SAL        NUMBER(7,2)    NOT NULL,
COMM       NUMBER(7,2),
DEPTNO     NUMBER(2)      NOT NULL
);

CREATE TABLE DEPT (
DEPTNO     NUMBER(2)      NOT NULL,
DNAME      VARCHAR2(14)   NOT NULL,
LOC        VARCHAR2(13)   NOT NULL
);
```

Figure 9: Correct Table Design

Therefore with many smaller, properly normalized and related table designs, you'll quite often need to glue together or "*join*" one or more of those related tables to construct the full or complete business data that you're after. In other words you'll need to project from more than one table to construct the desired and complete output. For that the basic SELECT syntax is expanded upon as follows (with the new clauses indicated in bold).

SELECT

{table|alias.}* |

{table|alias.}column_1

{ , **{table|alias.}**column_2 ... }

FROM **table_1 {{AS} alias_1}**

{ , table_2 {{AS} alias_2} ... }

{ WHERE

{{table_1|alias.}column_1 =

{table_2|alias.}column_2

...}

{ AND condition(s) } }

The above syntax is referred to as the "*implicit*" JOIN SQL coding style. It is considered by many as legacy and out of vogue. However it is still commonly used by people and many software tools generate their SQL code in this style – so it's still wise to be able to read it. Using our properly designed (i.e. normalized) EMP and DEPT tables from Figure 9, here's the implicit JOIN syntax to display the same output as in Figure 8 that was based upon the one big and poorly designed table. Examine the implicit join syntax here in Figure 10 closely – there is quite a lot going on in this one simple example.

```
SELECT a.*,
       b.dname, b.loc
FROM EMP a, DEPT b
WHERE a.deptno = b.deptno;
```

Figure 10: Implicit JOIN Example

One golden rule when doing any join is to make sure that you specify the proper number and type of join conditions. There should be a join condition between the parent primary key and the child foreign key for the table count minus one listed in the FROM clause. Moreover if those keys are composites (i.e. have multiple columns), then there will also be a additional condition per that key column count. If you skip the join conditions altogether or even just incorrectly specify them, the database will by default perform a "*Cartesian JOIN*" – which is simply every row from one table mindlessly joined to every row from the other. You almost never, ever want such a join because there is no real business logic or rationale for these row combinations. So always avoid a Cartesian JOIN!

One sure way to avoid such mistakes is to use the newer and preferred ASNI JOIN syntax. For that the basic SELECT syntax is expanded upon as follows (with the new clauses indicated in bold).

```
SELECT
  {table|alias.}* |
  {table|alias.}column_1
  { , {table|alias.}column_2 ... }
  FROM table_1 {{AS} alias_1}
  { {INNER |
    {FULL|LEFT|RIGHT} OUTER}
    JOIN
    table_2 {{AS} alias_2} ON
    { table_1|alias.}column_1 =
        {table_2|alias.}column_2
    ...}
  ... }
  { WHERE condition(s) } }
```

The above syntax is referred to as the "ex*plicit*" JOIN SQL coding style. Since the WHERE conditions and JOIN logic are now separated, it becomes a little clearer during SQL coding as to what is needed and when. Note the optional **INNER** keyword. By default database joins combine only the rows from both sides or tables that fully satisfy the join condition expressions. Any rows from either side or table that fail to meet those conditions are excluded.

Say you want to see the department names and their employee counts, but only for those departments that have employees currently working for them. Therefore an inner join between EMP and DEPT is needed as shown below in Figure 11. Note that this example uses both the INNER JOIN and GROUP BY features of the SELECT statement. We've now reached the point where doing anything useful with a SELECT command is going to require using multiple syntactical features. That's all right because in reality that's the type of SQL code you most often be writing.

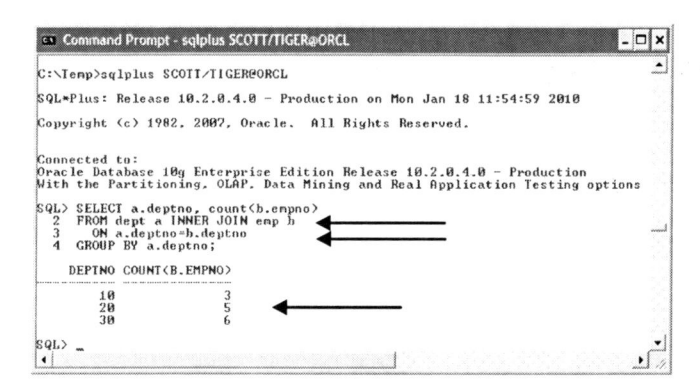

```
C:\Temp>sqlplus SCOTT/TIGER@ORCL
SQL*Plus: Release 10.2.0.4.0 - Production on Mon Jan 18 11:54:59 2010
Copyright (c) 1982, 2007, Oracle.  All Rights Reserved.

Connected to:
Oracle Database 10g Enterprise Edition Release 10.2.0.4.0 - Production
With the Partitioning, OLAP, Data Mining and Real Application Testing options

SQL> SELECT a.deptno, count(b.empno)
  2  FROM dept a INNER JOIN emp b
  3  ON a.deptno=b.deptno
  4  GROUP BY a.deptno;

    DEPTNO COUNT(B.EMPNO)
---------- --------------
        10              3
        20              5
        30              6

SQL>
```

Figure 11: INNER JOIN Example

Advanced SQL

But there is an interesting business question here – do these results tell the whole story? Maybe you really wanted to see the department names and their employee counts for all departments no matter what – even if no one works there. Therefore an outer join between EMP and DEPT is needed as shown below in Figure 12.

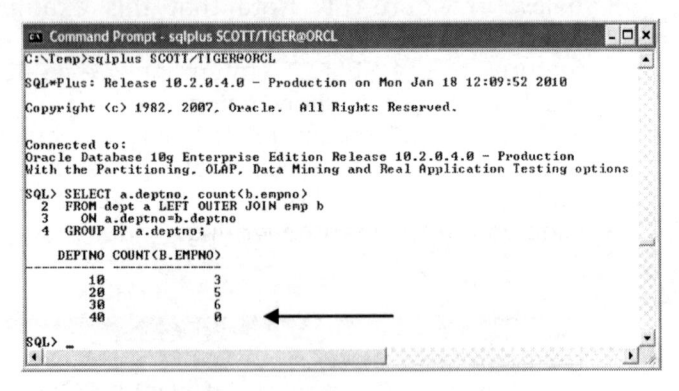

```
C:\Temp>sqlplus SCOTT/TIGER@ORCL

SQL*Plus: Release 10.2.0.4.0 - Production on Mon Jan 18 12:09:52 2010

Copyright (c) 1982, 2007, Oracle.  All Rights Reserved.

Connected to:
Oracle Database 10g Enterprise Edition Release 10.2.0.4.0 - Production
With the Partitioning, OLAP, Data Mining and Real Application Testing options

SQL> SELECT a.deptno, count(b.empno)
  2  FROM dept a LEFT OUTER JOIN emp b
  3  ON a.deptno=b.deptno
  4  GROUP BY a.deptno;

    DEPTNO COUNT(B.EMPNO)
---------- --------------
        10              3
        20              5
        30              6
        40              0

SQL>
```

Figure 12: OUTER JOIN Example

The fact that there is a department 40 and that no one works there might be critical information. Hence the outer join is the more business correct way to write this query as it exposes all the truth. Therefore think about what the business needs to see or know as you write your joins, you may find that in many cases the outer join is the better choice. There is a popular myth that outer joins are less efficient or slower than inner joins. They are not. Besides who cares – even if they were slower, the right answer is what's needed.

So what do the LEFT (as in Figure 12), RIGHT and FULL OUTER JOIN qualifiers do? They simply specify which side of the JOIN or table to include even if there are no matching rows from the other side or table. Therefore in Figure 12 LEFT simply means to include the DEPT rows even though no employees may work there. In other words include left side rows no matter what. FULL would simply include both sides (i.e. the equivalent of specifying both LEFT and RIGHT at the same time).

Sub-SELECT's

Thus far all the SELECT command examples are merely but a single, simple select operation. Even with JOIN's and all the other advanced syntax, there is still just one select operation being performed per command. But there are times when you may need to nest one SELECT operation within another – known as sub-SELECT's or sub queries. For that the basic SELECT syntax is expanded upon as follows (with the new clause indicated in bold).

```
SELECT ...
FROM ...
WHERE ...
    condition =|IN (SELECT ...)
    { AND condition(s) } }
    { GROUP BY ... }
    { HAVING ... }
    { ORDER BY ...}
```

This expanded syntax supports answering business questions like what is the average pay per person in the department that has the most employees? Let's construct this sub-query incrementally starting with the query shown in here Figure 13, which simply returns the total number of employees (across the whole company and thus all departments), and their average total compensation or pay.

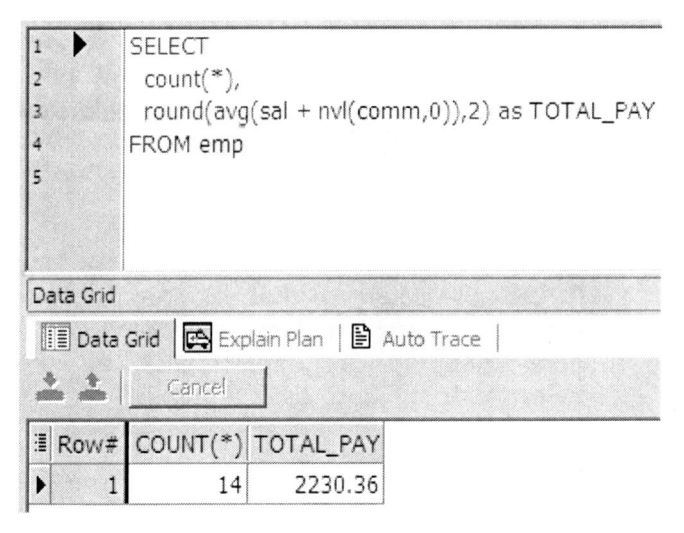

```
SELECT
  count(*),
  round(avg(sal + nvl(comm,0)),2) as TOTAL_PAY
FROM emp
```

Row#	COUNT(*)	TOTAL_PAY
1	14	2230.36

Figure 13: Sub Query Attempt #1

Note that this example introduced using two new built-in SQL functions upon the data returned. The NVL function is for handling optional or NULL values. Remember that anytime you include a NULL value in an expression or calculation, the result will always equal NULL. Thus to add together the employee's mandatory salary and optional commission, we must tell the database that any NULL commission values should be instead returned as zeros. Finally we used the ROUND function to display the resulting calculated number with a scale of 2 (i.e. two digits to the right of the decimal point).

However note that the SELECT in Figure 13 returns just one row for the average pay for all employees across all departments – and not just the one having the most employees. That's clearly not the answer that we're after.

So let's add the department number and a GROUP BY clause so that we now display the employee counts and their average pay per department for all departments, as shown below here in Figure 14.

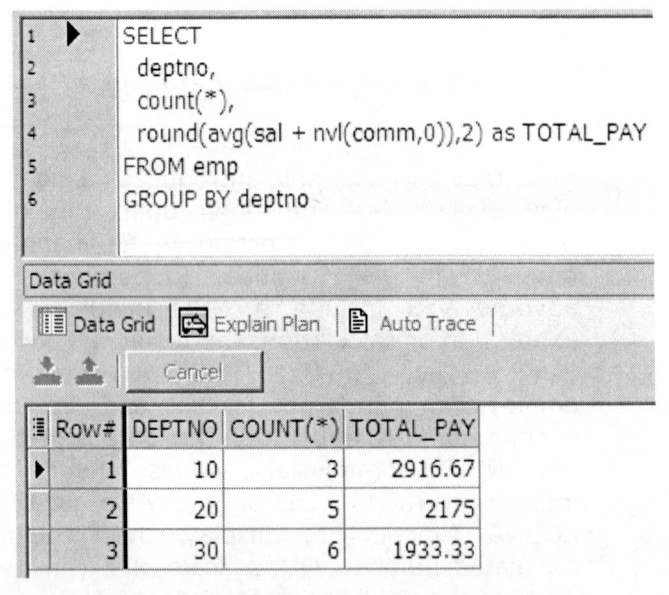

```
SELECT
    deptno,
    count(*),
    round(avg(sal + nvl(comm,0)),2) as TOTAL_PAY
FROM emp
GROUP BY deptno
```

Row#	DEPTNO	COUNT(*)	TOTAL_PAY
1	10	3	2916.67
2	20	5	2175
3	30	6	1933.33

Figure 14: Sub Query Attempt #2

However note that the SELECT in Figure 14 now returns one row per department for the average pay for all of its employees. While in this example it's easy enough to see that the correct answer is department 30 with 6 people each making an average of $1933.33, the database nonetheless had to all the work and display the results for each and every department. Therefore if there had been 1,000 departments, the total amount of internal processing performed would have greatly exceeding what was needed for just the one row of interest. Plus we would have had to manually look at all 1,000 department rows returned to decide which was the correct answer.

We could now cheat as shown here in Figure 15 and now return the same rows but now in ascending sorted order – since we know the first row will be the correct one and then simply ignore all of the remaining rows.

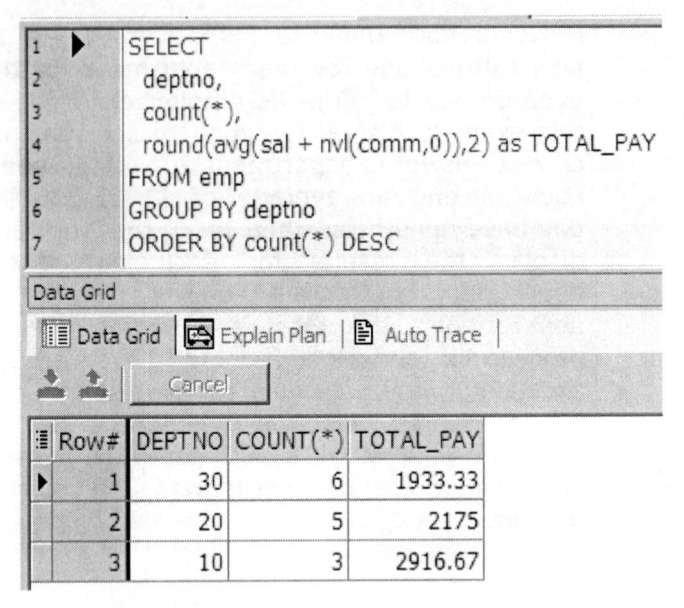

```
1 ▶  SELECT
2      deptno,
3      count(*),
4      round(avg(sal + nvl(comm,0)),2) as TOTAL_PAY
5   FROM emp
6   GROUP BY deptno
7   ORDER BY count(*) DESC
```

Row#	DEPTNO	COUNT(*)	TOTAL_PAY
1	30	6	1933.33
2	20	5	2175
3	10	3	2916.67

Figure 15: Sub Query Attempt #3

But once again the internal processing expended to process the other non-answer departments (e.g. 999 others) would represent a huge waste of computer resources – and possibly slow the database for everyone else for no extra insights.

The way to solve this is to embed one SELECT command inside another. Think "divide and conquer", which is to say solve bigger problems in smaller, more understandable and thus manageable parts. The SELECT back from Figure 13 labeled "Sub Query Attempt #1" would work (i.e. provide the right answer) if we knew that department 30 was the correct department, and we could thus simply provide a WHERE clause explicitly stating this restriction as shown here in Figure 16. So think of this missing query to provide that now hard coded WHERE clause value as the sub query to nest or embed within this SELECT statement. That's what we'll be developing next, the sub-SELECT to return the department with the most employees.

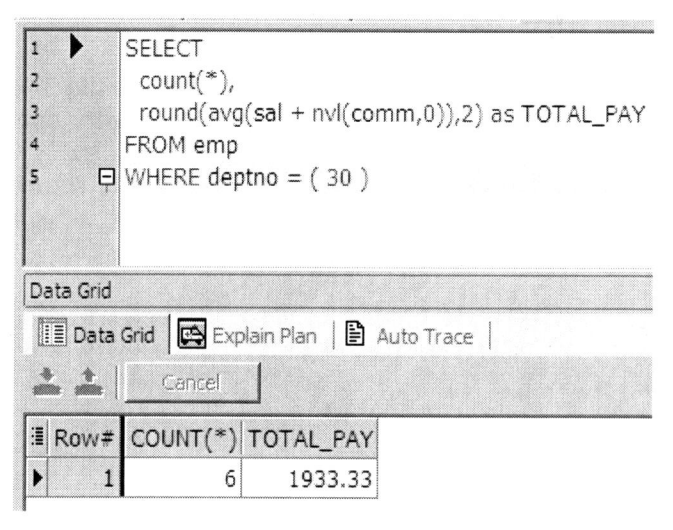

```
SELECT
   count(*),
   round(avg(sal + nvl(comm,0)),2) as TOTAL_PAY
FROM emp
WHERE deptno = ( 30 )
```

Row#	COUNT(*)	TOTAL_PAY
1	6	1933.33

Figure 16: Sub Query Attempt #4

So how do we query the database to find the "TOP N" rows that satisfy our search criteria. Some databases provide a very simple SELECT syntax for this problem, such as the following examples in Figure 17.

```
Microsoft SQL Server

SELECT TOP 10 column FROM table

PostgreSQL and MySQL

SELECT column FROM table
LIMIT 10
```

Figure 17: TOP-N Query Examples

However Oracle does not offer such a simple and direct SELECT syntax for obtaining TOP-N results. Instead you have to use a very special syntactical construct called an "inline view" and the RANK function as shown here in Figure 18.

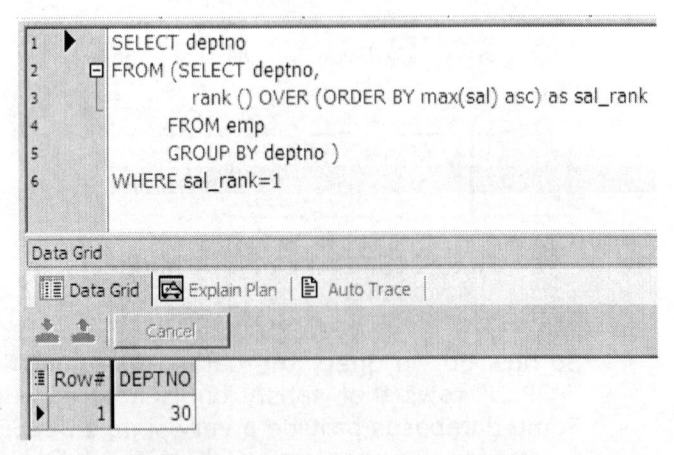

```
1  SELECT deptno
2  FROM (SELECT deptno,
3           rank () OVER (ORDER BY max(sal) asc) as sal_rank
4        FROM emp
5        GROUP BY deptno )
6  WHERE sal_rank=1
```

Data Grid | Explain Plan | Auto Trace

Row#	DEPTNO
1	30

Figure 18: Inline View Example

Introduction to Oracle

While an "inline view" may look very much like a sub-SELECT, it's actually not. Refer back to the syntax template at the start of this section and you'll see that sub-SELECT's are handled in the WHERE clause. In Figure 18 we have a sub-SELECT, but it's in the FROM clause. So technically speaking the "inline view" is really something a little different. But sometimes people will refer to this construct as well as a type of sub-SELECT. That's OK.

So putting together all we've learned and incrementally built in this section, we end up with the query shown here in Figure 19.

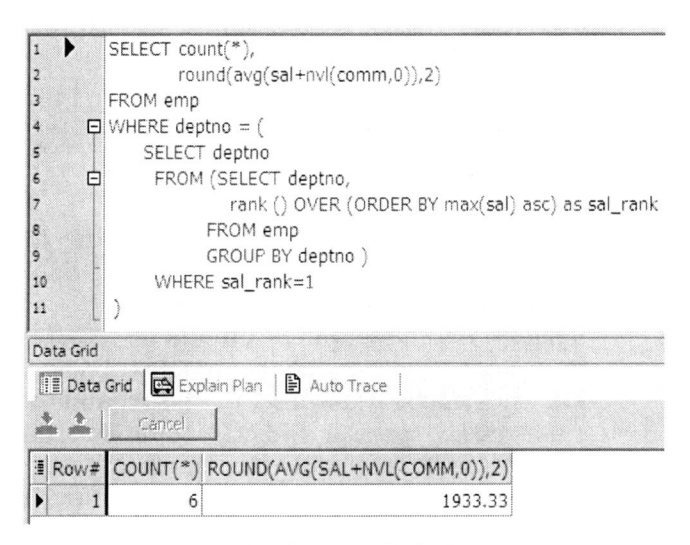

```
1   SELECT count(*),
2          round(avg(sal+nvl(comm,0)),2)
3   FROM emp
4   WHERE deptno = (
5       SELECT deptno
6       FROM (SELECT deptno,
7               rank () OVER (ORDER BY max(sal) asc) as sal_rank
8             FROM emp
9             GROUP BY deptno )
10      WHERE sal_rank=1
11  )
```

Row#	COUNT(*)	ROUND(AVG(SAL+NVL(COMM,0)),2)
1	6	1933.33

Figure 19: Correct Sub Query

Advanced SQL

While you might feel that the syntax for this correct answer seems a little overly complex, it nonetheless returns the correct business result and for big databases (e.g. many departments) it does the minimal amount of work that's required. Thus this solution is both effective and efficient.

Don't let the complexity of the syntax bother you – as most SQL commands that truly answer real world business questions will be this complex or more. While there might be some very basic business questions properly answered with trivial SQL like examples in prior chapters, the bulk of genuinely useful SQL commands will require coding efforts more like those in this chapter – and specifically this last section.

Conclusion

In this chapter we covered some of the more involved but extremely useful SELECT command constructs and their syntax. The SELECT command varies greatly in complexity from very simple to highly complex. Using just the constructs presented in this chapter one could easily write a SELECT command that's several pages in length to return the correct results for but a single business question. And that query could include multiple SELECT command constructs from this chapter –

including joins, outer joins, sub-SELECT's and "inline views".

Chapter 7: SQL Developer

Working with a database is similar in some general respects to driving an automobile as shown in the table below.

	Automobile Trip	**Database Work**
Infra Structure	Highway	Computer System
Guide	Road Map	Data Dictionary
Tool	Automobile	SQL Developer

Note the two cells near the bottom right corner – Data Dictionary and SQL Developer. SQL Developer is a free, graphical user interface (i.e. GUI) tool from Oracle for making database work very easy. And for any database, the data dictionary is simply the road map to its contents – meaning the table, index and view definitions.

SQL Developer will actually serve as both your database tool and road map. Thus you will both investigate how the database is structured and access its data using this one tool. This chapter will cover the key basic tasks which SQL Developer makes easy. However it can do much more.

Note – SQL Developer also supports third party software vendor plug-ins. Therefore it can and has been extended to perform many more tasks and operations than covered here.

Install

Beginning with Oracle version 11g, SQL Developer is part of the basic client install (refer back to Chapter 2). For prior versions, you have to manually download and unzip the roughly 100MB file – and place a shortcut on your desktop to the SQL Developer executable. For most of you who are more current (i.e. using the latest and greatest Oracle versions), SQL Developer will automatically and simply be located under the Windows Start menu as Programs -> Oracle -> Application Development as shown here in Figure 1.

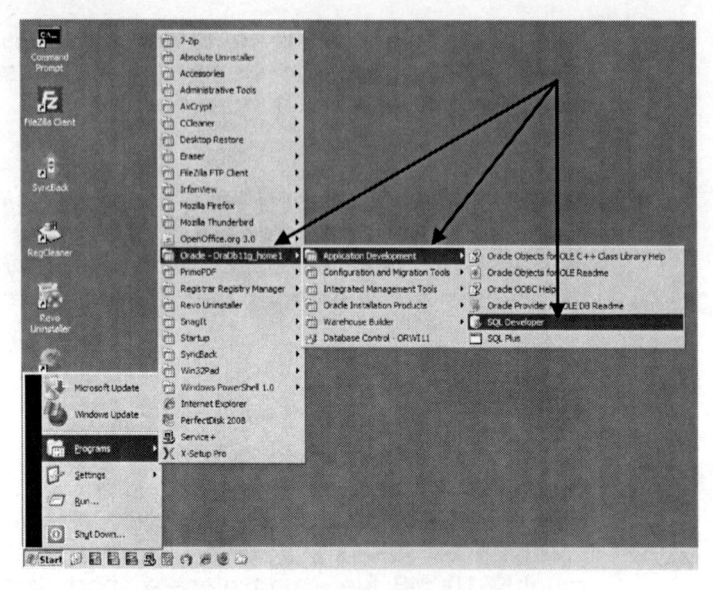

Figure 1: Launching SQL Developer

Connecting

In order to work with any database you must first create or establish a connection – often referred to as *"logging on"* to the database (refer back to Chapter 3). For that you simply choose from the SQL Developer main menu File -> New -> Connection or press the plus sign (i.e. +) toolbar icon, both of which launch the database connection screen shown here in Figure 2.

Introduction to Oracle

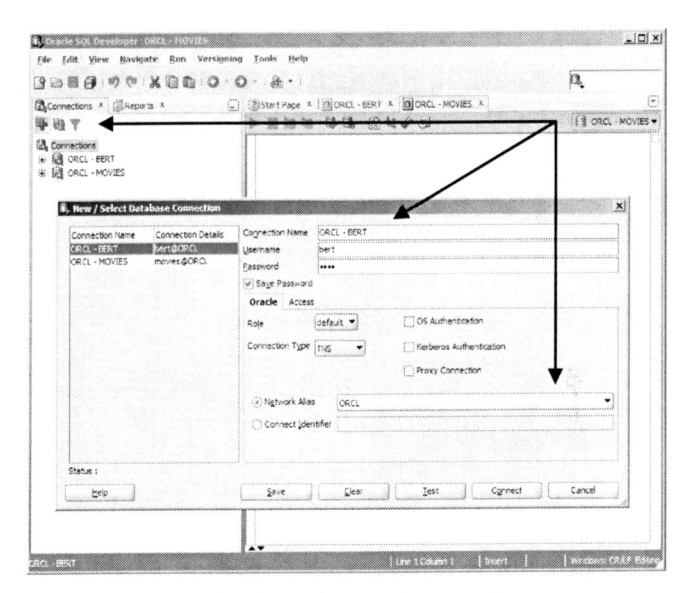

Figure 2: Creating a Connection

You simply provide an alias name for the connection (i.e. the name you'll refer to it by) and then provide the requisite connection information: user name, password and database alias – which is the database name or SID defined in your TNSNAMES.ORA file (refer back to Chapters 2 and 3). In fact the drop-down box for the *"Network Alias"* will be populated by reading your TNSNAMES.ORA file.

Once a database connection has been defined and made, it will then show up under "Connections" on the left hand side of the screen. From that point on you can now

SQL Developer **105**

connect to that database by any of three methods:

- Right Hand Mouse -> Connect
- Double Click on the Connection
- Expand the Node (i.e. click on +)

Browsing

One of the most basic and useful tasks in working with any database is to investigate or "*snoop around*" to see what's available (i.e. tables, views, etc). Of course if you already know the database or have at least worked with it some, you may do less browsing. But when you first start working with a new database, browsing may well be the chief activity that you perform.

SQL Developer's left hand side of the screen contains a tree-view referred to as the "*Connections Navigator*" which makes all database browsing trivially easy. When you connect to the database, this navigator expands to show you all the database object types available to you as shown in Figure 3.

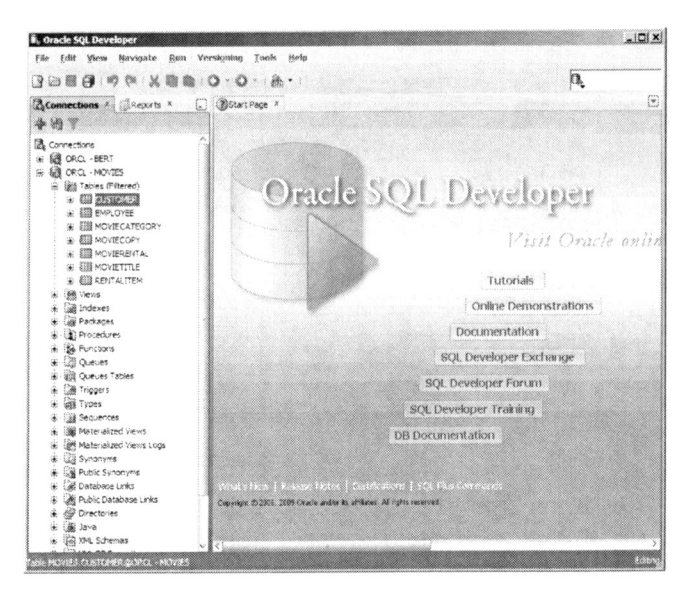

Figure 3: Connections Navigator

While SQL Developer calls this tree-view the "*Connections Navigator*", you may hear people refer to it as either the database explorer or database browser. But by whatever name you call it, it provides our "*road map*" to the database. You will therefore browse the database's meta-data or data dictionary using this facility.

Once you double click on or select a named object, such as the CUSTOMER table, SQL Developer will display a new worksheet or tab on the right hand side with the details for that object as shown here in Figure 4.

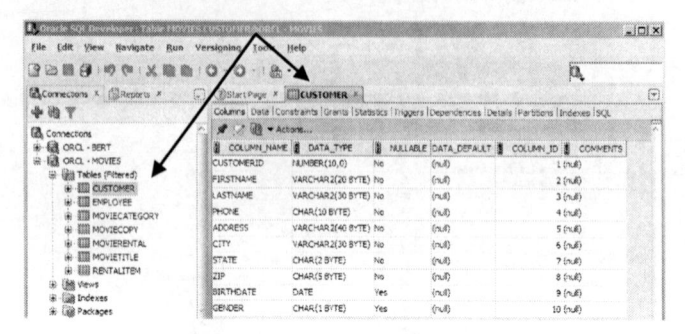

Figure 4: Table Details

Note that there are sub-tabs under that main tab – such as *"Columns"*, *"Data"*, *"Constraints"*, etc. When you double click on a table, by default the first tab will display that table's column information. Thus you can see their column names, data types, default values and whether they are optional or mandatory. The two sub-tabs that you'll use most will likely be *"Data"* and *"SQL"*.

The *"SQL"* sub-tab simply displays the Data Definition Language (i.e. DDL) for the object as shown in Figure 5 – in this case the table and its indexes. You can of course select, and cut/paste this SQL code as needed.

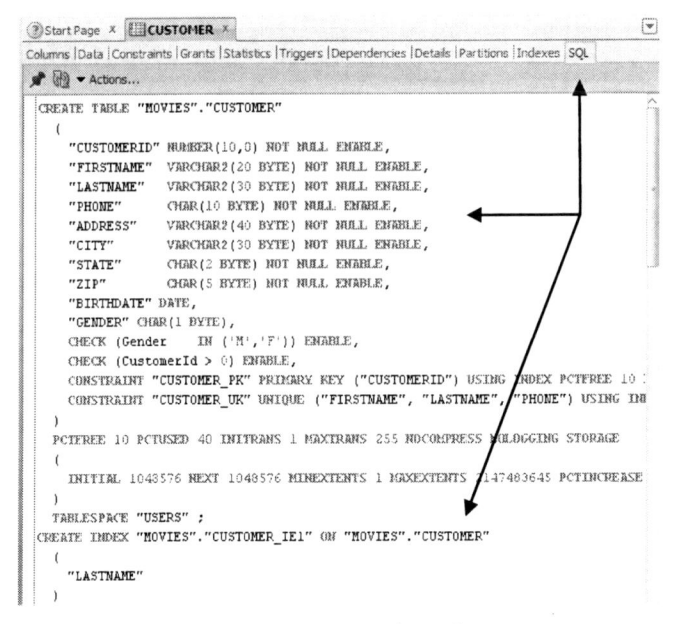

```
Start Page    CUSTOMER
Columns | Data | Constraints | Grants | Statistics | Triggers | Dependencies | Details | Partitions | Indexes | SQL
     Actions...
CREATE TABLE "MOVIES"."CUSTOMER"
  (
    "CUSTOMERID" NUMBER(10,0) NOT NULL ENABLE,
    "FIRSTNAME"  VARCHAR2(20 BYTE) NOT NULL ENABLE,
    "LASTNAME"   VARCHAR2(30 BYTE) NOT NULL ENABLE,
    "PHONE"      CHAR(10 BYTE) NOT NULL ENABLE,
    "ADDRESS"    VARCHAR2(40 BYTE) NOT NULL ENABLE,
    "CITY"       VARCHAR2(30 BYTE) NOT NULL ENABLE,
    "STATE"      CHAR(2 BYTE) NOT NULL ENABLE,
    "ZIP"        CHAR(5 BYTE) NOT NULL ENABLE,
    "BIRTHDATE"  DATE,
    "GENDER"     CHAR(1 BYTE),
    CHECK (Gender   IN ('M','F')) ENABLE,
    CHECK (CustomerId > 0) ENABLE,
    CONSTRAINT "CUSTOMER_PK" PRIMARY KEY ("CUSTOMERID") USING INDEX PCTFREE 10
    CONSTRAINT "CUSTOMER_UK" UNIQUE ("FIRSTNAME", "LASTNAME", "PHONE") USING IN
  )
  PCTFREE 10 PCTUSED 40 INITRANS 1 MAXTRANS 255 NOCOMPRESS NOLOGGING STORAGE
  (
    INITIAL 1048576 NEXT 1048576 MINEXTENTS 1 MAXEXTENTS 2147483645 PCTINCREASE
  )
  TABLESPACE "USERS" ;
CREATE INDEX "MOVIES"."CUSTOMER_IE1" ON "MOVIES"."CUSTOMER"
  (
    "LASTNAME"
  )
```

Figure 5: SQL Sub-Tab

The "Data" sub-tab displays the table's actual data as shown in Figure 6 – and may well be the one SQL Developer feature that you use and rely upon the most. Because it's simply that useful.

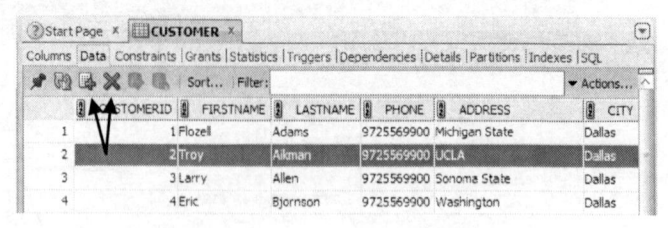

Figure 6: Data Sub-Tab

The toolbar icons of a sheet of paper with a green plus sign and the red X allow you to add and/or delete rows respectively. As the Troy Aikman row is highlighted in Figure 6, pressing the red X will result in that row being "*marked as deleted*", indicated by a minus sign prefix on the row number, as shown here in Figure 7.

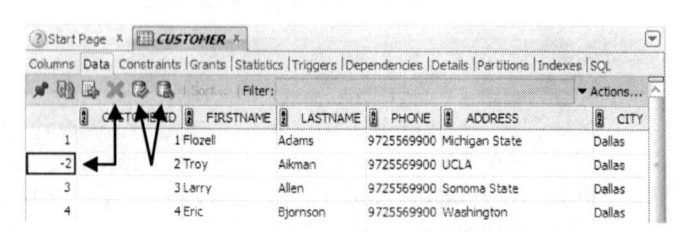

Figure 7: Deleting Rows

Note that the toolbar icons for the red X is now disabled, and the disks with a green check and a red backwards arrow are now enabled. These last two toolbar icons represent commit and rollback respectively. The changes will be made to the database and

110 Introduction to Oracle

visible to all other users if committed, and will revert to the original data if rolled back.

Of course since most tables have far more rows than once can effectively view and work with, SQL Developer provides a simple filter mechanism to restrict the rows display shown here in Figure 8 – think of this as simply a WHERE clause appended to a SELECT upon the table.

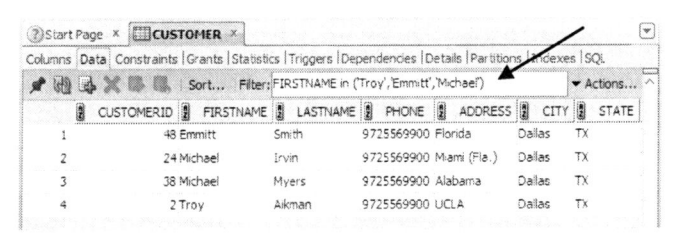

Figure 8: Filtering the Data

Thus to display only the rows for customers with the first name of Troy, Emmitt and Michael, we simply add the SQL code for that restriction. You may have noticed that the customers are Dallas Cowboys players and this restriction attempted display just the trio of famous players often referred to as the triplets. Of course as you can see this restriction was insufficient as a fourth player also had a first name of Michael. That's how data mining often goes – you try different things until you find the right combination.

SQL Developer

Often when viewing the table data, you'll want to sort the results to make them easier to scan, comprehend and digest. By pressing the "*Sort*" button a pop-up window will permit you to specify one or more column to sort upon as shown here in Figure 9. Once you've selected the sort columns, note how they will be prefixed with an up arrow for ascending, a down arrow for descending and a number as to their sort order.

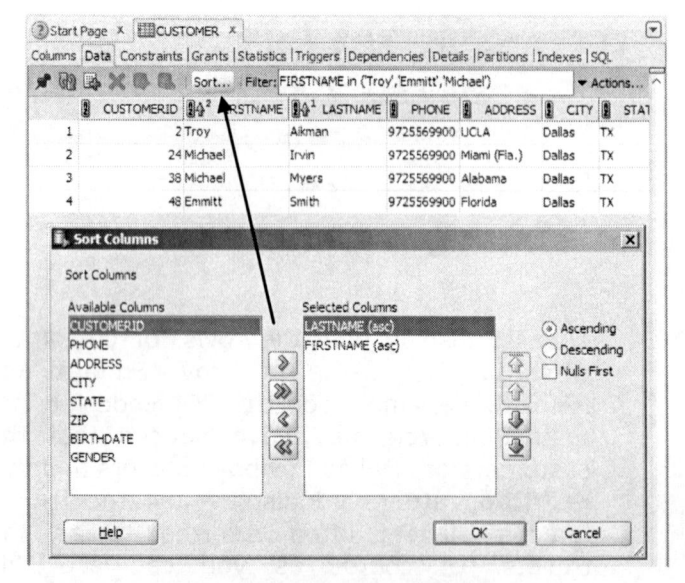

Figure 9: Sorting the Data

Once you've found the data that you're after, it's time to do something with it. In many cases you'll simply want to get a copy to work with in some other tool. For example to export this data into a Microsoft Excel spreadsheet, you now simply open or expand the "*Actions*" drop-down and choose Export Data > xls as shown here in Figure 10.

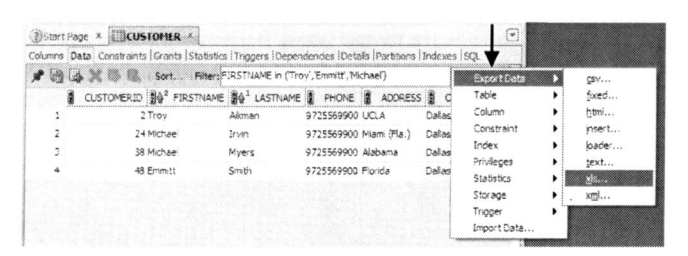

Figure 10: Exporting the Data

SQL Developer will open the data export pop-up shown in Figure 11. You can export to a file or the clipboard.

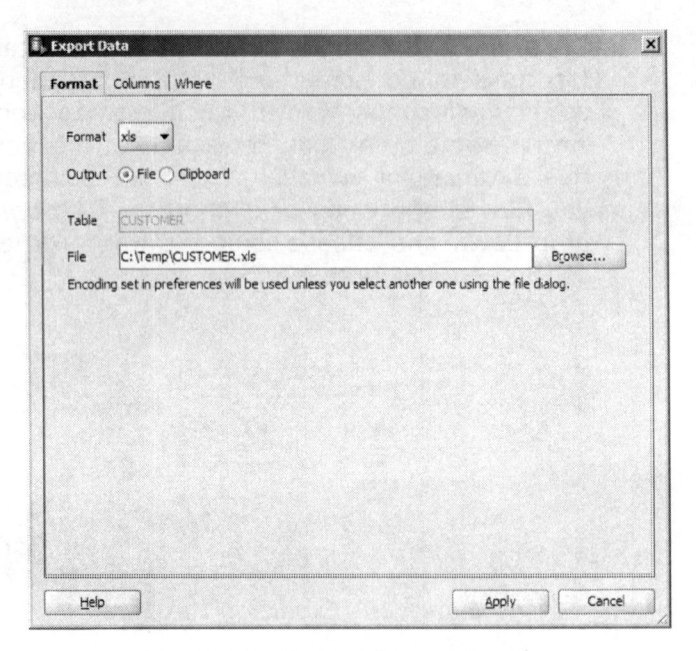

Figure 11: Export Data Wizard

Note the "*Columns*" and "*Where*" tabs. By default SQL Developer will export all the columns and rows – regardless of your filtering. So you may want to specify what projection and restriction to apply. Note however that the sort order specified will apply to the export.

Querying

When you first connect to a database, SQL Developer will automatically open a SQL

Worksheet for that connection as shown here in Figure 12.

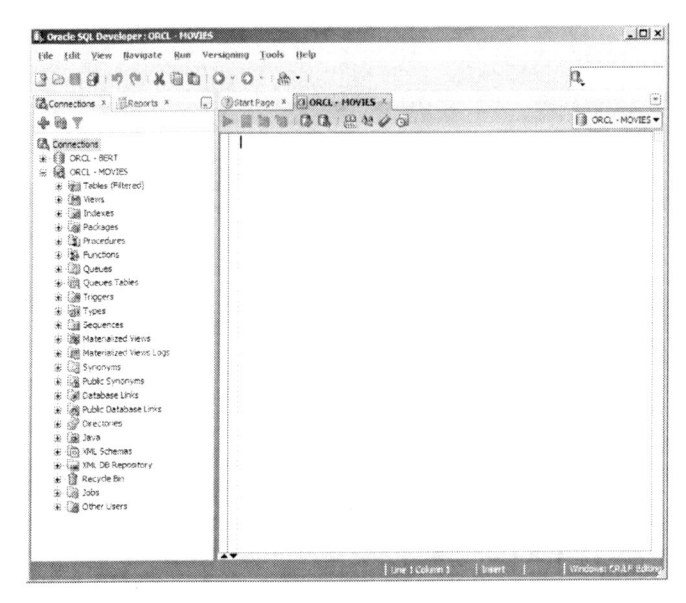

Figure 12: SQL Worksheet

This SQL Worksheet is simply a SQL editing facility much like Windows Notepad – except that it understands the SQL language (i.e. performs syntax highlighting). Once your type some SQL code the Window will activate additional toolbar icons as shown here Figure 13.

SQL Developer **115**

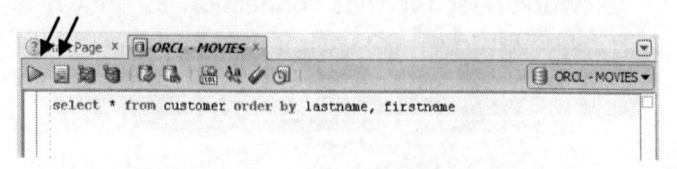

Figure 13: Query Entered

The first two toolbar icons, the green triangle and the sheet of paper with a green triangle, represent the "*Execute*" and "Execute as Script" SQL command execution options respectively.

The "*Execute*" toolbar icon and its Control-Enter keyboard shortcut simply mean to run the command and display the results in a data grid exactly like the Connection Navigator in the prior section. Thus the results (i.e. data grid) will appear as shown here in Figure 14.

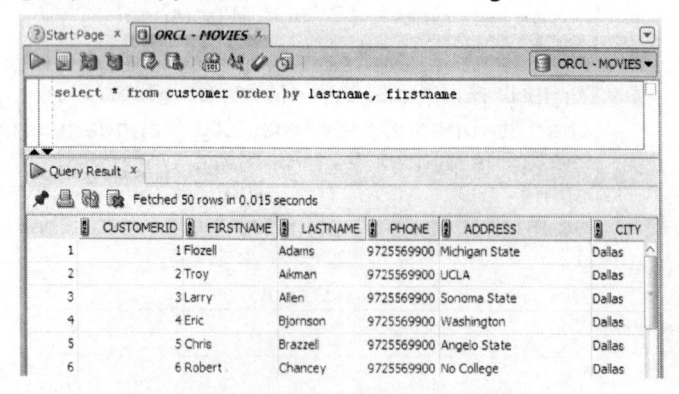

Figure 14: Execute

116 Introduction to Oracle

Note that the newly added "Query Result" section appears very similar to the "*Connection Navigator's Data*" sub-tab back in Figure 6 – minus most of the toolbar icons, sort button, filter box and actions drop-down. However some of those actions (e.g. export data) are available via the right hand menu as shown in Figure 15. That's why the "Connection Navigator" was covered first – because you need to know about the database objects to work with them, and the "Execute" works the same as the right hand side object tab's "Data" sub-tab.

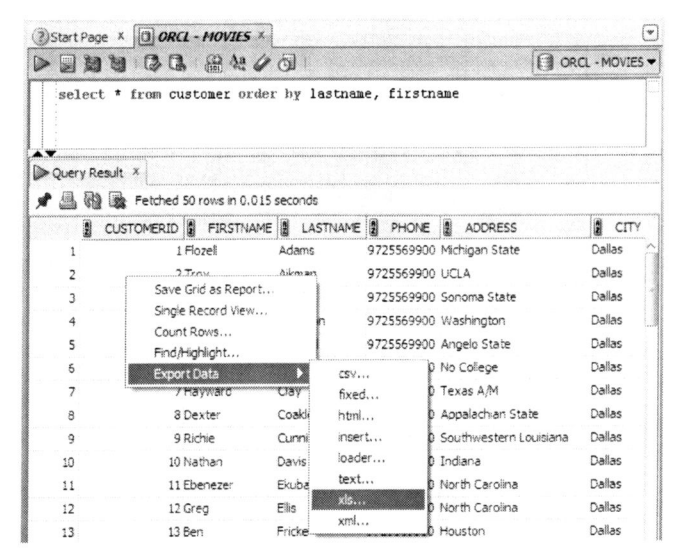

Figure 15: Data Grid Right-Hand-Menu

SQL Developer

The "*Execute as Script*" toolbar icon and its F5 keyboard shortcut simply mean to run the command and display the results as if it had been run in SQL*Plus as a script. Thus the results (i.e. text output) will appear as shown here in Figure 16. There are toolbar icons to save this output to a text file or print it – however there are no right hand menu options for any other type of operations. Of course you can select and cut/paste like any text area.

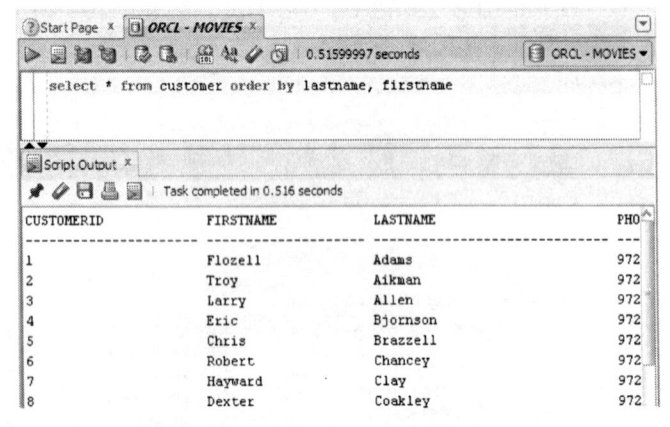

```
select * from customer order by lastname, firstname

Task completed in 0.516 seconds
CUSTOMERID          FIRSTNAME            LASTNAME                        PHO
----------          ---------            --------                        ---
1                   Flozell              Adams                           972
2                   Troy                 Aikman                          972
3                   Larry                Allen                           972
4                   Eric                 Bjornson                        972
5                   Chris                Brazzell                        972
6                   Robert               Chancey                         972
7                   Hayward              Clay                            972
8                   Dexter               Coakley                         972
```

Figure 16: Execute as Script

Conclusion

In this chapter we covered the very basics of Oracle's SQL Developer graphical user interface tool – namely connecting, browsing and querying the database. These activities will most likely represent 80% or more of what most people do on a regular basis. And with this basic introductory knowledge, any user should be able to investigate further and eventually master SQL Developer. As a free tool (with the Oracle client install), SQL Developer is a great asset when working with any Oracle database – as it makes users much more productive. It lets you concentrate on what you need to do rather than how to do it.

Chapter 8: TOAD

This chapter will cover the same topics as the last, but this time on Quest Software's TOAD for Oracle (often just called TOAD) rather than Oracle's SQL Developer. While SQL Developer is free, it's only been around for a couple years now – and is on version 2.X. Whereas TOAD has been around for well over a decade and is on version 10.X. Since TOAD was the only real good tool for a long time, many shops and people have standardized on it. So even though SQL Developer is free, they have long history and investment in TOAD – and thus cannot switch. As such, there are some million people worldwide using TOAD. Therefore no book teaching Oracle would be complete without a chapter on TOAD.

Note – Quest Software offers TOAD for Oracle as both a freeware available on www.toadsoft.com and as a pay-for commercial product. The commercial version offers numerous additional features and several bundles for various roles – such as analyst, developer and DBA.

Install

TOAD freeware and commercial are both regular Windows programs that are installed like any other – i.e. via an executable (i.e. EXE) file or Microsoft installer (i.e. MSI) file, depending on the TOAD version. Depending on your Windows Vista and Windows 7.0 User Access Control (i.e. UAC) settings, you may have perform the install using a user in the administrators group.

The TOAD freeware times out every sixty days and requires that no more than five people per company use it. When the freeware expires, you simply download a zip file with an updated exe and unzip that file in your TOAD install directory. You do not have to get the full installer and perform a complete install each time.

Connecting

In order to work with any database you must first create or establish a connection – often referred to as "*logging on*" to the database (refer back to Chapter 3). For that you simply choose from the TOAD main menu Session -> New Connection or press the plug with a blue plus sign (i.e. +) toolbar icon, both of which launch the database login screen shown here in Figure 1.

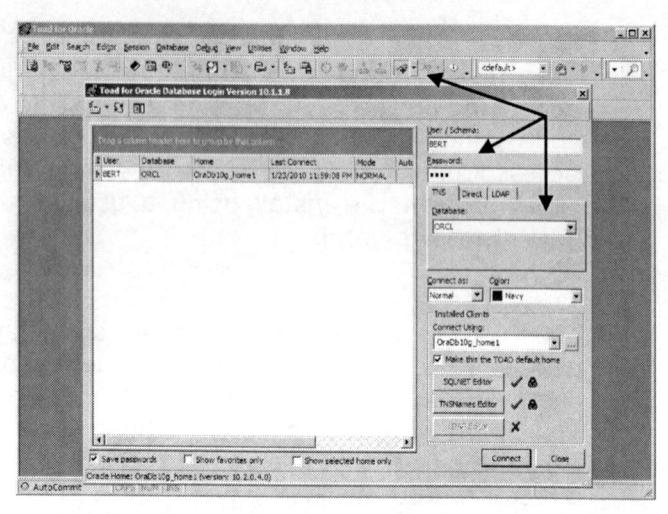

Figure 1: Creating a Connection

You simply provide the requisite connection information: user name, password and database alias – which is the database name or SID defined in your TNSNAMES.ORA file (refer back to Chapters 2 and 3). In fact the drop-down box for the "*Database*" will be populated by reading your Oracle Home's TNSNAMES.ORA file.

Once a database connection has been defined and made, TOAD will then automatically open whatever screen you've defined in its plethora of options – by default it will open an occurrence of the "*Editor*".

Browsing

One of the most basic and useful tasks in working with any database is to investigate or "*snoop around*" to see what's available (i.e. tables, views, etc). Of course if you already know the database or have at least worked with it some, you may do less browsing. But when you first start working with a new database, browsing may well be the chief activity that you perform.

TOAD has a "Schema Browser" screen which makes all database browsing trivially easy. You launch it either via the main menu Sessions -> Schema Browser of by pressing the Schema Browser toolbar icon (i.e. a database and tree-view together). The Schema Browser expands to show you all the database object types available to you as shown in Figure 2.

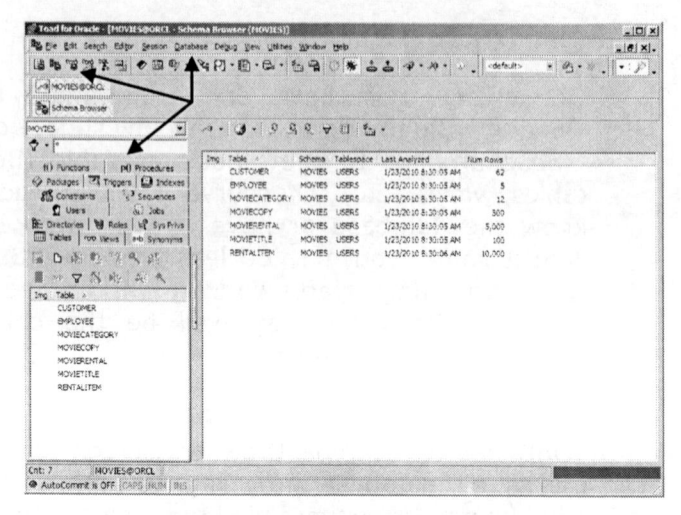

Figure 2: Schema Browser

While TOAD calls this tree-view the *"Schema Browser"*, you may hear people refer to it as either the database explorer or database browser. But by whatever name you call it, it provides our *"road map"* to the database. You will therefore browse the database's meta-data or data dictionary using this facility.

Once you single click on or select a named object on the right hand side, such as the CUSTOMER table, TOAD will display a set of tabs on the right hand side with the details for that object as shown here in Figure 3.

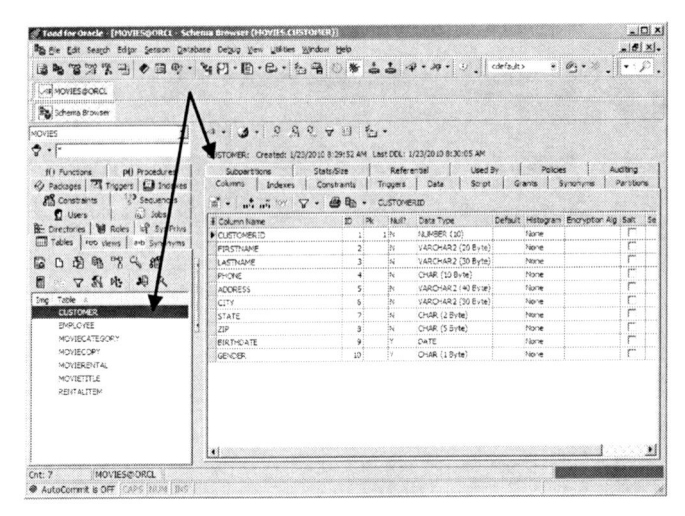

Figure 3: Table Details

Note that there are many right hand side tabs – such as *"Columns"*, *"Data"*, *"Constraints"*, etc. When you click on a table, by default the first tab will display that table's column information. Thus you can see their column names, data types, default values and whether they are optional or mandatory. The two other right hand side tabs that you'll use most will likely be *"Data"* and *"Script"*.

The *"Script"* right hand side tab simply displays the Data Definition Language (i.e. DDL) for the object as shown in Figure 4 – in this case the table and its indexes. You can of course select, and cut/paste this SQL code as needed.

Microsoft Office **125**

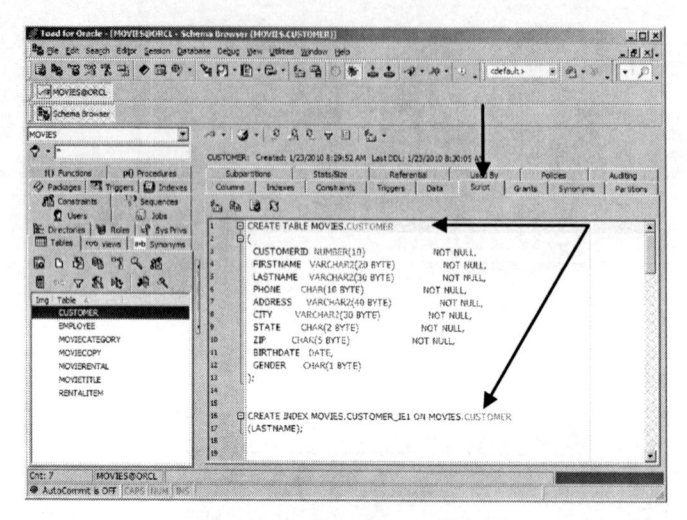

Figure 4: SQL Sub-Tab

The "Data" right hand side tab displays the table's actual data as shown in Figure 5 – and may well be the one TOAD feature that you use and rely upon the most. Because it's simply that useful.

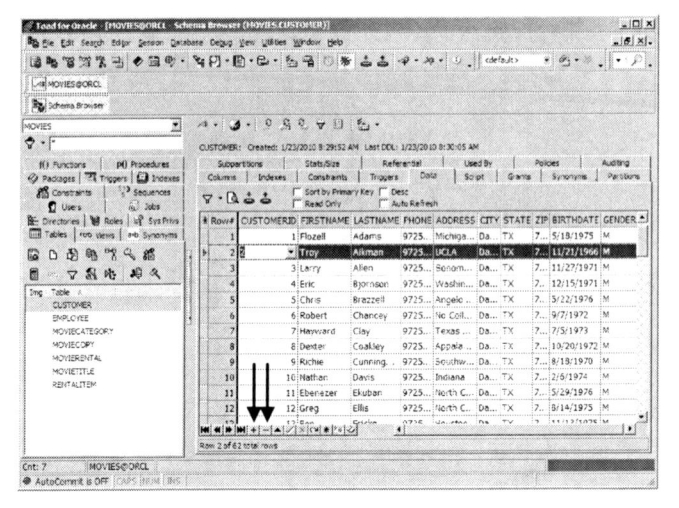

Figure 5: Data Sub-Tab

The bottom navigator icons of plus (i.e. +) and minus (i.e. -) signs allow you to add and/or delete rows respectively. As the Troy Aikman row is highlighted in Figure 6, pressing the minus sign will result in that row being deleted from the data grid, but it won't be real until you press the commit icon. The changes will be made to the database and visible to all other users if committed, and will revert to the original data if rolled back.

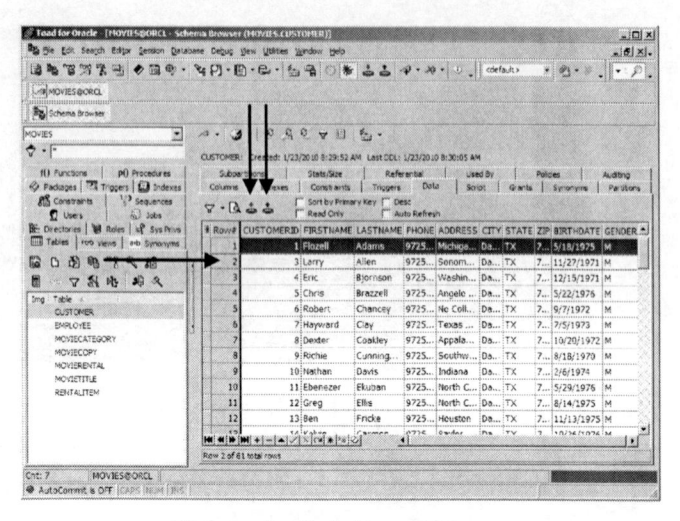

Figure 6: Deleting Rows

Of course since most tables have far more rows than once can effectively view and work with, TOAD provides a simple filter mechanism to restrict the rows displayed – the funnel toolbar icon. When the funnel is grey, no filters are in force. When red, then there are filters in force restricting the data rows returned. Pressing the funnel launches the sort/filter screen shown here in Figure 7 – think of this as simply a WHERE clause appended to a SELECT upon the table.

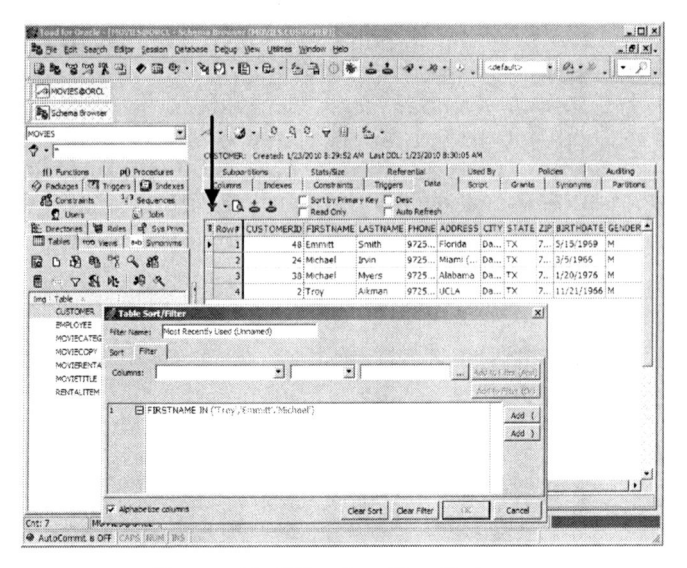

Figure 7: Filtering the Data

Thus to display only the rows for customers with the first name of Troy, Emmitt and Michael, we simply add the SQL code for that restriction. You may have noticed that the customers are Dallas Cowboys players and this restriction attempted display just the trio of famous players often referred to as the triplets. Of course as you can see this restriction was insufficient as a fourth player also had a first name of Michael. That's how data mining often goes – you try different things until you find the right combination.

Often when viewing the table data, you'll want to sort the results to make them easier to scan, comprehend and digest. By pressing the funnel toolbar icon a pop-up window will permit you to specify one or more column to sort upon as shown here in Figure 8. Once you've selected the sort columns, note how the funnel icon now also includes a blue halo or crown.

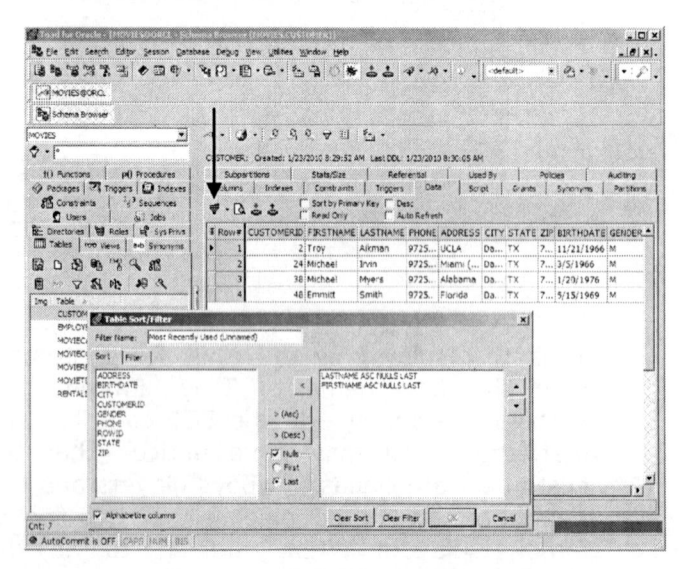

Figure 8: Sorting the Data

Once you've found the data that you're after, it's time to do something with it. In many cases you'll simply want to get a copy to work with in some other tool. For example to export this data into a Microsoft Excel spreadsheet, you now simply mouse onto the data grid, press the right hand mouse, and then choose "*Export Dataset*" as shown in Figure 9.

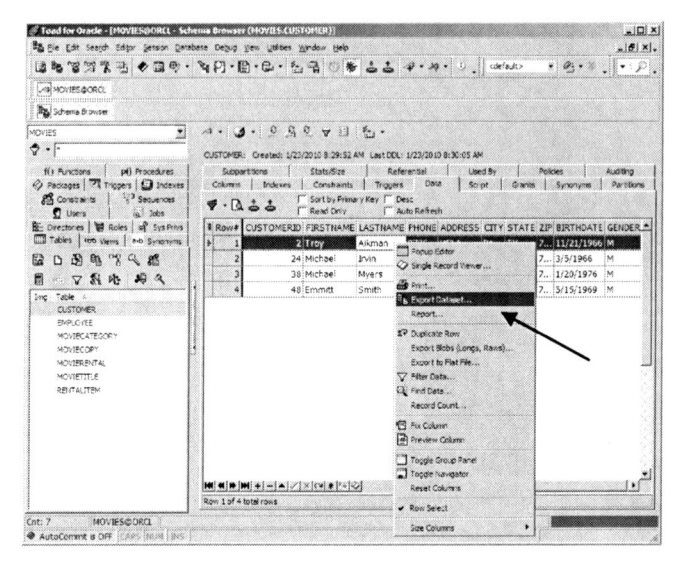

Figure 9: Exporting the Data

TOAD will open the data export pop-up shown in Figure 10. You can export to a file or the clipboard.

Microsoft Office **131**

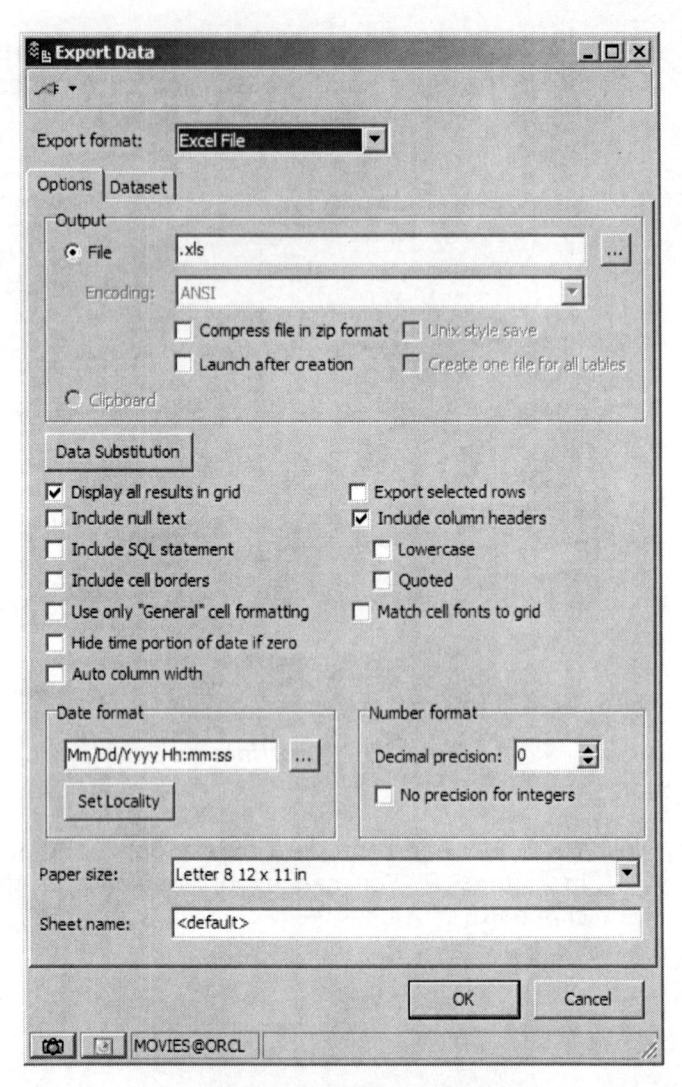

Figure 10: Export Data Wizard

Note the "*Dataset*" tab. By default TOAD will export all the columns and rows currently displayed in the grid. So you may want to specify what projection and restriction to apply. The "*Dataset*" tab will contain the complete SELECT command required for the export – which you can then modify.

Querying

When you first connect to a database, TOAD will automatically open a SQL Editor for that connection as shown here in Figure 11.

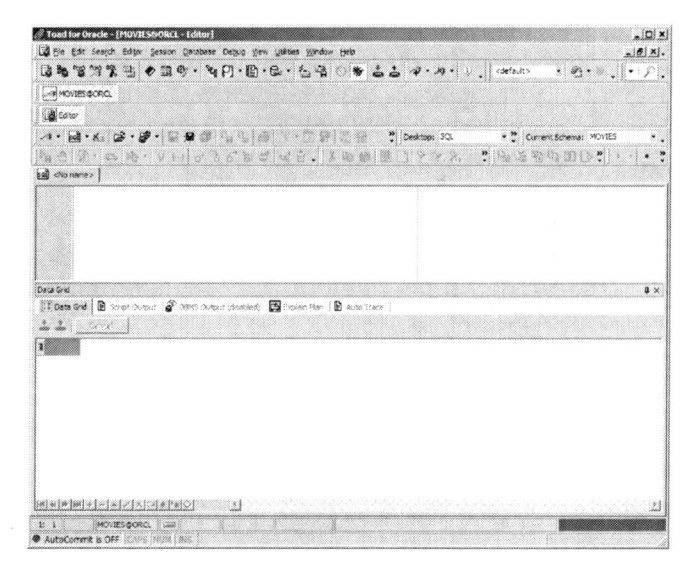

Figure 11: SQL Worksheet

Microsoft Office **133**

This SQL Editor is simply a SQL editing facility much like Windows Notepad – except that it understands the SQL language (i.e. performs syntax highlighting). Once type some SQL code the Window will activate additional toolbar icons as shown here Figure 12.

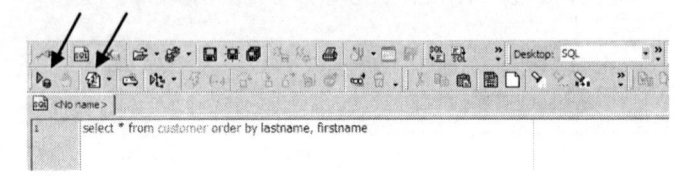

Figure 12: Query Entered

The first and third toolbar icons, the green triangle with disk and the sheet of paper with a lightning bolt, represent the "*Execute*" and "Execute as Script" SQL command execution options respectively.

The "*Execute*" toolbar icon and its F9 keyboard shortcut simply mean to run the command and display the results in a data grid exactly like the Schema Browser in the prior section. Thus the results (i.e. data grid) will appear as shown here in Figure 13.

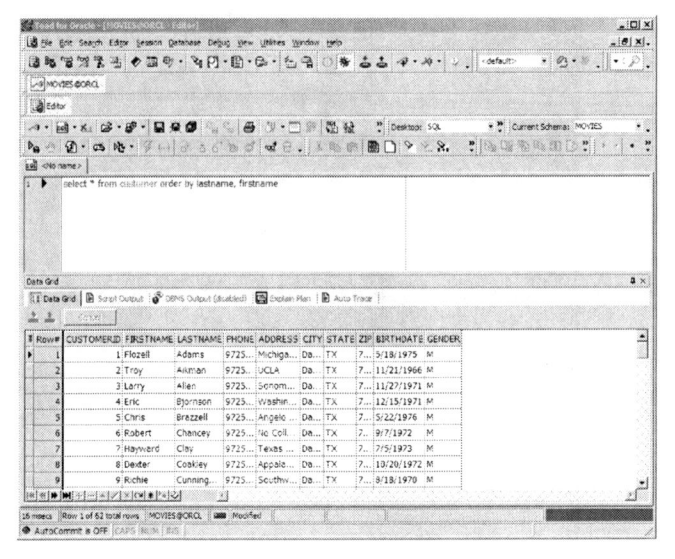

Figure 13: Execute

Note that the newly added "Data Grid" section appears very similar to the "Schema Browser's Data" right hand side tab back in Figure 5 – minus most of the toolbar icons, sort button, filter box and actions drop-down. However some of those actions (e.g. export data) are available via the right hand menu as shown in Figure 14. That's why the "Schema Browser" was covered first – because you need to know about the database objects to work with them, and the "Execute" works the same as the "Data" right hand side tab.

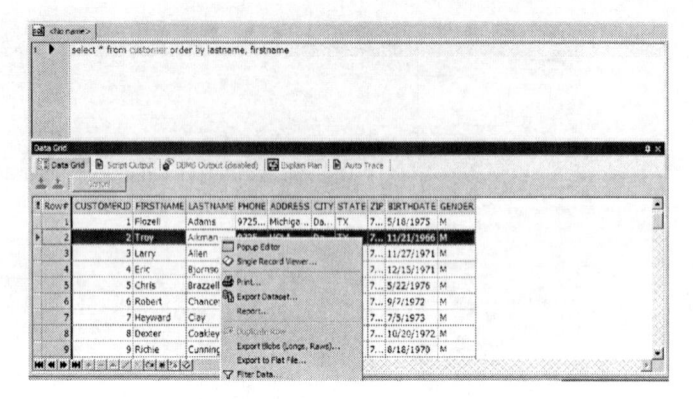

Figure 14: Data Grid Right-Hand-Menu

The "*Execute as Script*" toolbar icon and its F5 keyboard shortcut simply mean to run the command and display the results as if it had been run in SQL*Plus as a script. Thus the results (i.e. text output) will appear as shown here in Figure 15. There are toolbar icons to save this output to a text file or print it – however there are no right hand menu options for any other type of operations. Of course you can select and cut/paste like any text area.

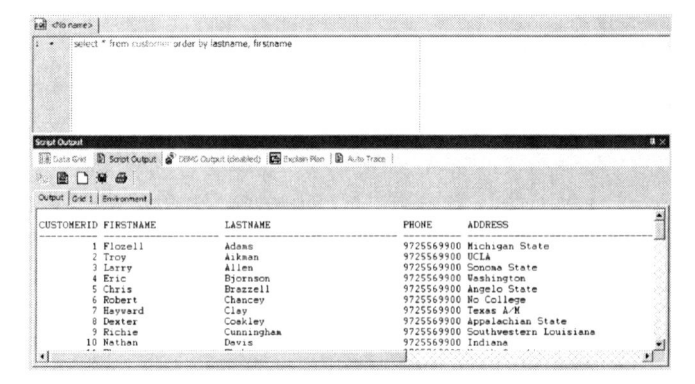

Figure 15: Execute as Script

Conclusion

In this chapter we covered the very basics of Quest Software's TOAD graphical user interface tool – namely connecting, browsing and querying the database. These activities will most likely represent 80% or more of what most people do on a regular basis. And with this basic introductory knowledge, any user should be able to investigate further and eventually master TOAD. Both the TOAD freeware and commercial versions are great assets when working with any Oracle database – as it makes users much more productive. It lets you concentrate on what you need to do rather than how to do it.

Chapter 9: Microsoft Office

Let's face it – for corporate desktops Microsoft Office has a near monopoly. Most workers, from information systems geeks to frontline business users, have some version of Microsoft Office on their PC. And as was shown in the past two chapters, many people will use database tools like SQL Developer and TOAD to export the data they need into other tools, such as Microsoft Excel or Access. Here we'll learn how to utilize your Oracle database directly from within your Microsoft Office tools. Because some of you will be able to skip the interim tool and export once you see how to do it from within Microsoft Office.

MS Excel

Business people have become experts or "*gurus*" on Microsoft Excel. So much so that many business analysts have become essentially Excel application developers and/or programmers. Some business people use their information system people simply to find and export their Oracle data for them, which they then perform their magic on using Excel. But Excel can directly access your Oracle database and it's not that hard to do.

Let's see how we'd get our CUSTOMER table data into a spreadsheet for further work. You start be choosing main menu's Data -> Import External Data -> New Database Query as shown here in Figure 1.

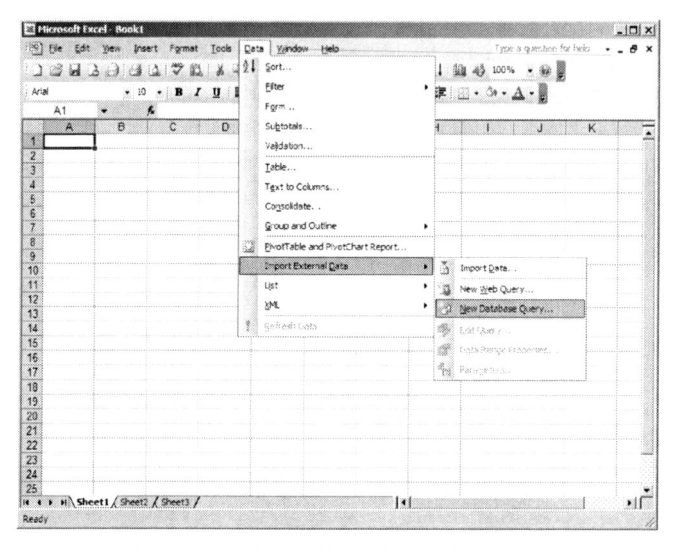

Figure 1: Excel Database Query

This will launch a little pop-up window as shown below in Figure 2 where you specify what ODBC data source to use for your database connection (refer back to Chapter 3 on how to set this up).

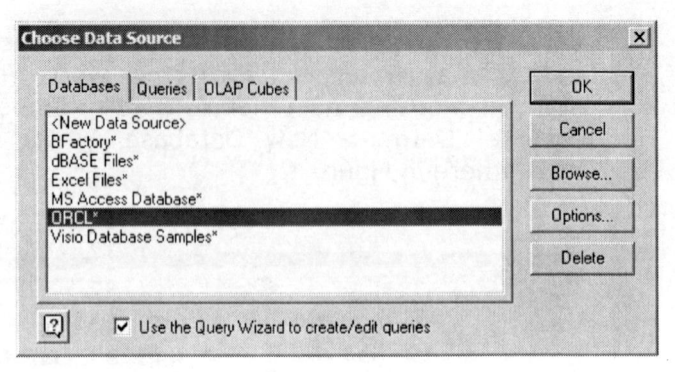

Figure 2: Choose ODBC Source

If the ODBC data source does not already have the database username and password information saved as part of its definition, then you will see the following login screen pop-up as shown here in Figure 3.

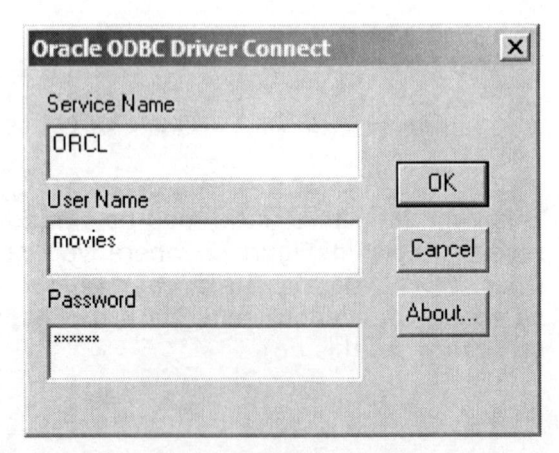

Figure 3: ODBC Login

140 Introduction to Oracle

Once you've established a successful connection to the database, you'll then see a query construction wizard as shown in Figure 4.

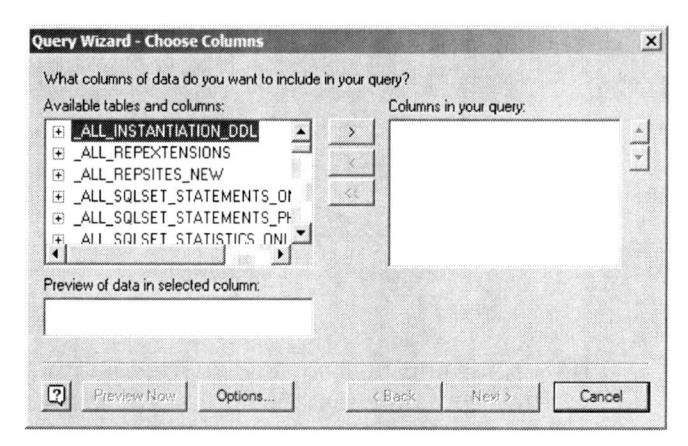

Figure 4: Overloaded Query Wizard

Note that when this wizard launches it will list every table in the database that you could select. So to reduce this information overflow, it's wise to press the "Options" button to launch the table options screen shown here in Figure 5. Using these options you can change the table owner from <ALL> to the schema or user whose tables you want to work with – and choose to just show the tables for that user.

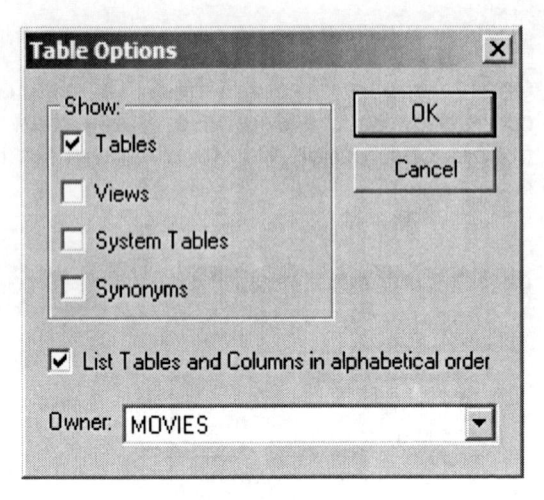

```
┌─ Table Options ──────────────────── X ┐
│  ┌─ Show: ──────────────┐   ┌──────┐  │
│  │  ☑ Tables            │   │  OK  │  │
│  │  ☐ Views             │   └──────┘  │
│  │                      │   ┌──────┐  │
│  │  ☐ System Tables     │   │Cancel│  │
│  │  ☐ Synonyms          │   └──────┘  │
│  └──────────────────────┘             │
│                                       │
│  ☑ List Tables and Columns in alphabetical order │
│  Owner: [MOVIES                    ▼] │
└───────────────────────────────────────┘
```

Figure 5: Table Options

Now returning back to the query construction wizard, the only database objects displayed will be the MOVIES schema's tables as shown here in Figure 6. Note that all the CUSTOMER tables columns were selected. Note too that the columns display in alphabetical order since I also chose that option on the prior screen.

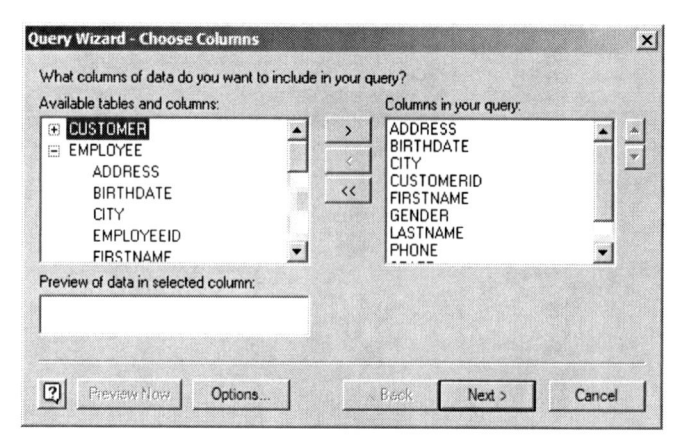

Figure 6: Workable Query Wizard

Next the query wizard will allow you to define any filters or restrictions that you want to place on the data. As with the prior chapter's examples, we want the customers whose first name is either Troy, Emmitt or Michael. That's accomplished by placing a three part filter on the first name and using the drop-down box to easily choose from the existing customers' first names as shown in Figure 7.

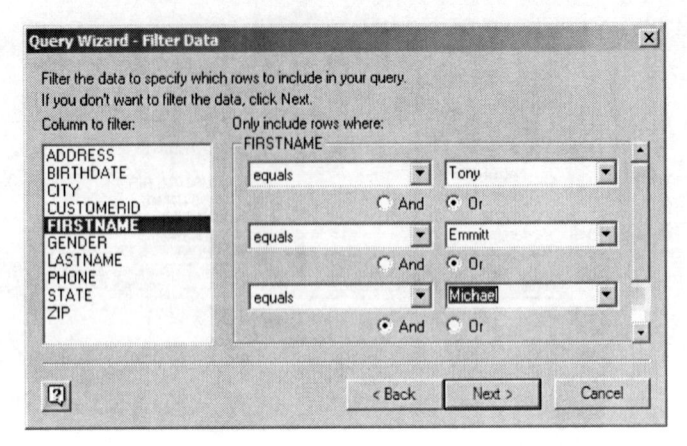

Figure 7: Query Filter

Now the query wizard permits defining any sorting you desire on the returned data as shown here in Figure 8.

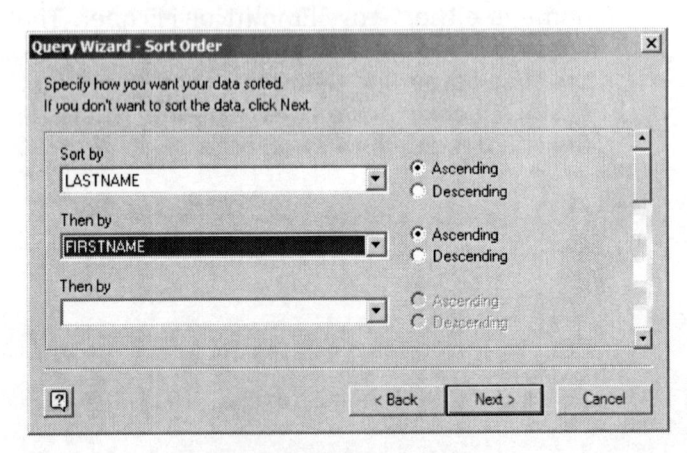

Figure 8: Query Sorting

Lastly the query wizard will prompt you to either return the data back into Excel, load the query into the query editor, or create an OLAP cube. The choices are shown here in Figure 9.

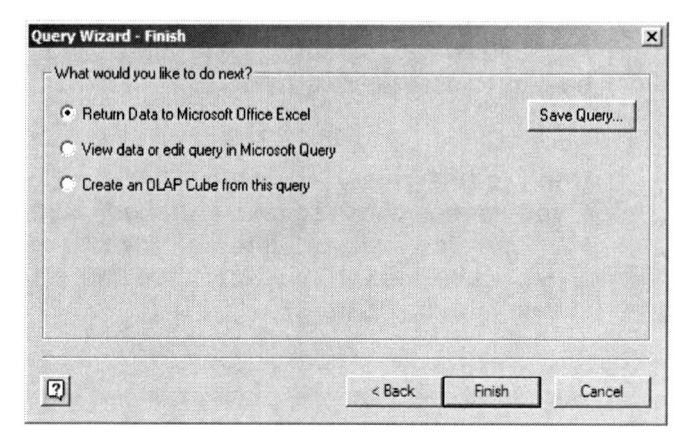

Figure 9: Query Completion

If you choose the first choice, you'll now see all your Oracle database rows and columns returned back into your spreadsheet.

Figure 10: Data Now in Excel

Microsoft Office

Again the beauty of this method is that you can avoid having to use other database tools like SQL Developer and TOAD to find and export the data for later importing back into Excel. You can do this all directly from within Excel itself – thereby saving time and not having to use multiple tools.

If in the final query wizard step back in Figure 9 you instead chose to take the query built for you by the wizard into a manual SQL construction area – you would see the screen shown here in Figure 11.

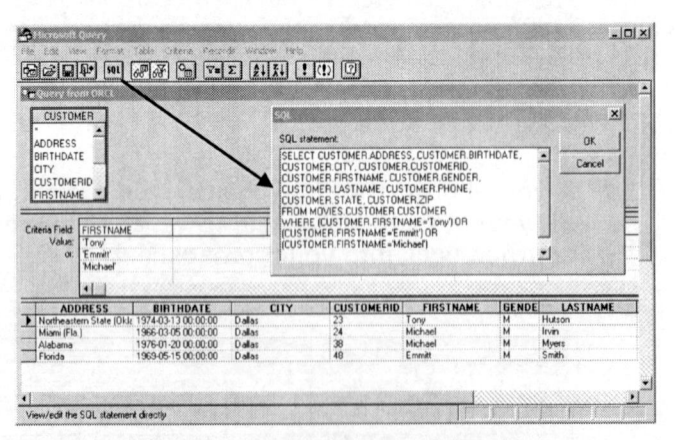

Figure 11: Manual Query Builder

The query builder screen is divided into three parts. The top section shows a picture or data model type diagram of the tables you're working on and any relationships between them. If you're familiar with Access, this will look familiar. The middle section provides a place to enter the restriction criteria – that which becomes your WHERE clause. And the bottom section shows the live data the query will return. If you then press the SQL button as shown in Figure 11, you'll see the pop-up window that displays the actual SQL code that has been constructed.

MS Access

For those lucky enough to have Microsoft Office Professional, you already have a top notch database tool that you can use – MS Access. Plus you can operate in one of two modes: work on the actual data in the Oracle database or make a local Access database copy to work with.

As with the prior section and Excel, you'll first need to have an Oracle ODBC data source defined on your machine (refer back to Chapter 3 on how to set this up).

You first choose main menu File -> Open or the folder icon on the toolbar. That will launch the typical Windows application file open screen. On that screen choose a file type of ODBC Databases, which is the last choice on the drop-down box. You'll then see the same pop-up screens as back in Figures 2 and 3 for the ODBC data source selection and database login.

Access will now display its database link definition screen as shown here in Figure 12. Here you can select all the Oracle tables and/or views that you want to be able to work with from within Access.

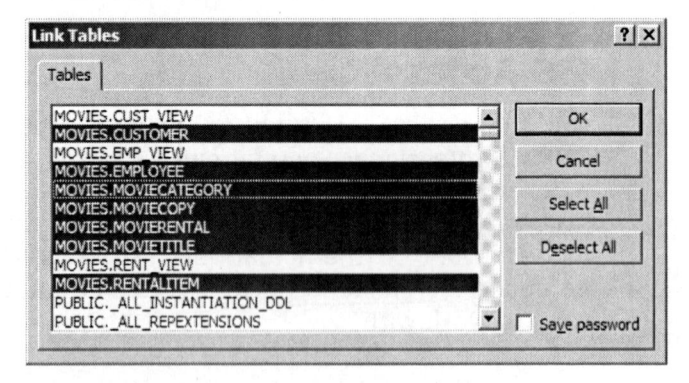

```
Link Tables                                            ? X
 Tables
   MOVIES.CUST_VIEW                    ▲      OK
   MOVIES.CUSTOMER
   MOVIES.EMP_VIEW                             Cancel
   MOVIES.EMPLOYEE
   MOVIES.MOVIECATEGORY
   MOVIES.MOVIECOPY                            Select All
   MOVIES.MOVIERENTAL
   MOVIES.MOVIETITLE                           Deselect All
   MOVIES.RENT_VIEW
   MOVIES.RENTALITEM
   PUBLIC._ALL_INSTANTIATION_DDL
   PUBLIC._ALL_REPEXTENSIONS           ▼     ☐ Save password
```

Figure 12: Table Link Selection

When you press the "*OK*" button be prepared to wait. You'll see a progress bar of sorts as Access reaches out to Oracle to both find and understand the database objects that you've selected. Once that process completes you'll see the typical Access database work options as shown here in Figure 13.

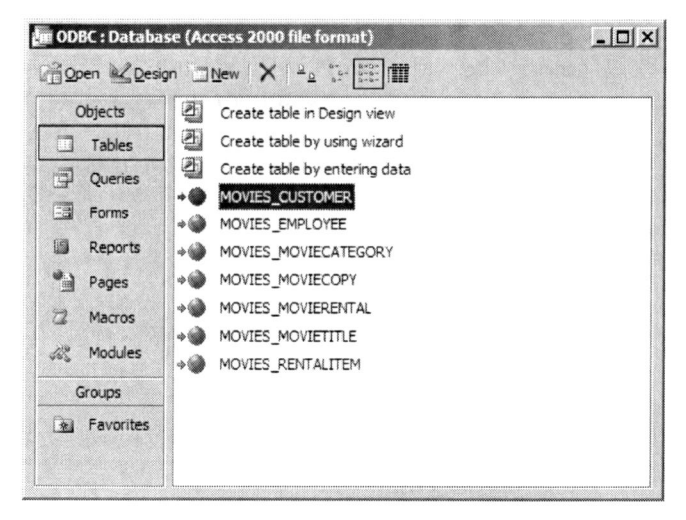

Figure 13: Access Links to Oracle

You'll notice the little arrow pointing to a globe icon next to each of the tables listed. This indicates that these are external tables with links to be worked upon via Access. So the Oracle tables and their data are still on the Oracle database server and not copied onto your PC.

You now can use any of Microsoft Access' tools and techniques to work with your data. However in this case it will simply be sending the SQL over to Oracle and fetching back the resulting rows. The local Access database files (i.e. ODBC.MDB) will only contain the meta-data and pointers to the Oracle database – and thus will be very small.

To make a local copy of the Oracle table you select the new table wizard toolbar icon and select import table as shown in Figure 14. You then choose the ODBC data source, provide the connection info and select the table(s) to be imported (i.e. copied locally) into your Access Database.

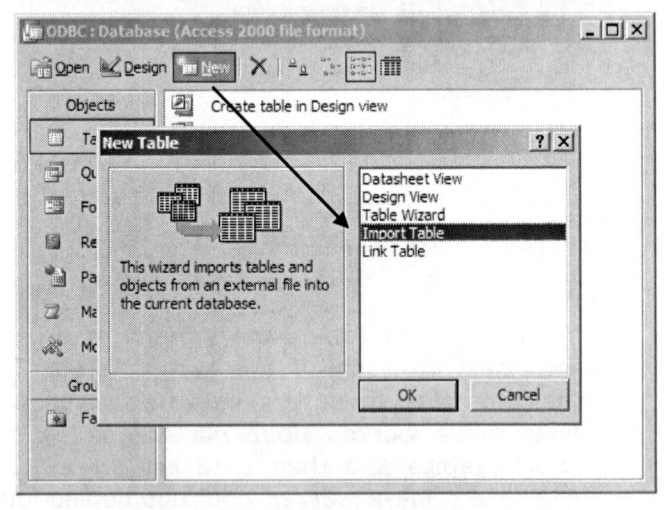

Figure 14: Importing Tables

When you're successfully completed the table import you'll now see a local copy of that table in your object list with a table icon (i.e. grid) next to it as shown in Figure 15.

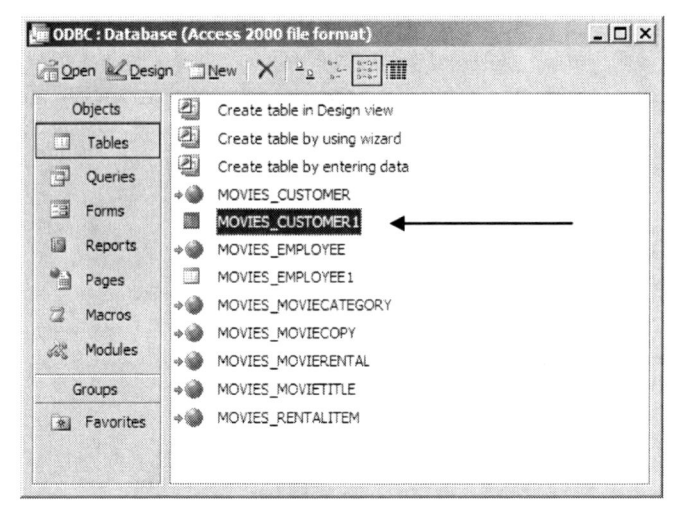

Figure 15: Local Copy of Table

Two items to note. First the bigger the table you import the longer it will take and the more network traffic it will cause. Second, your local hard drive better have sufficient room to host all the data that Oracle returns.

Conclusion

In this chapter we covered using your existing Microsoft Office tools to directly work with your Oracle database. Excel can link into your Oracle data via a query wizard and editor. Access can link to your tables as well as import them into local copies. Plus Access offers numerous other capabilities and tools which might assist with your work. For example building screens and reports in

Access is pretty straightforward and easy. So why attempt that work in some other database tool when you have perfectly good tools already on your PC that you know and use everyday already.

Chapter 10: Database Sandbox

Sometimes the quickest and best way to learn any new technology is to create a sandbox or playground type environment where you can try your new skills without worrying about impacting other people. Oracle offers its database for free download. There are three versions – Enterprise edition, Standard Edition, and Express Edition.

The Express Edition is a very simple to install, easy to use and easy to manage version of the Oracle database. It has most of the features of the standard edition, so it makes for an excellent learning arena. It does have some database size (4 GB) and computer resource limits (1GB RAM and 1 CPU) – but for basic Oracle experimentation and learning these limits should not be an issue. Plus the Express Edition is totally free, there are no options or requirements for any kind of purchase.

In fact the Oracle Express Edition data sheet on Oracle's web site states that:

Oracle Database XE is a great starter database for new administrators and educational institutions or students who need a database for their curriculum. It comes complete with management browser interface to monitor database activity and manage database users, storage, and memory. Since Oracle Database XE is built using the same code base as Oracle Database 10g Release 2 it provides flexibility for future growth. Applications developed and deployed using Oracle Database XE can easily be upgraded to Oracle Database 10g Standard Edition One, Standard Edition, and Enterprise Editions without any coding changes.

Installation

The Oracle Express Edition installer is a normal Windows application and is about 160 MB in size (whereas Oracle Enterprise Edition 11g is 1.8 GB). As with other windows installers you merely launch it and answer some fairly basic questions. That's it.

The Oracle Express installer will display about eight windows as part of the overall install process. Of those, only two are significant and thus worth note. The first screen of note allows you to specify the location where Oracle Express will be installed, as shown here in Figure 1. By default it places Oracle Express Edition in the directory "C:\ORACLEXE".

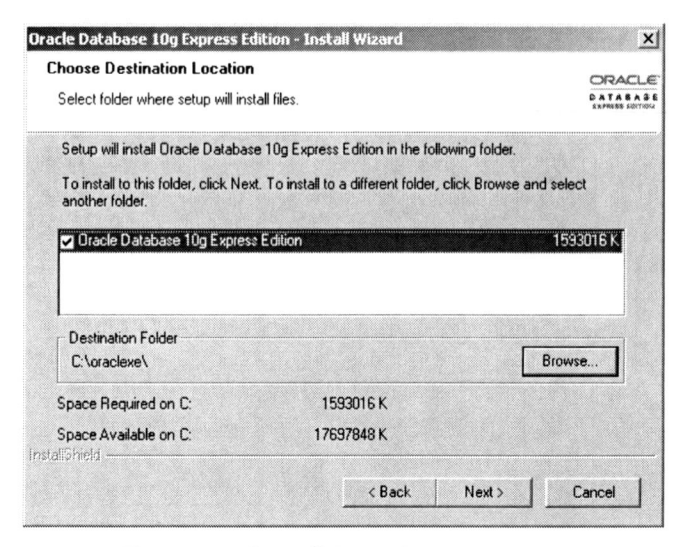

Figure 1: Install Location screen

The second installer screen of note allows you to specify the password for the default DBA user account in the starter database it creates, as shown here in Figure 2.

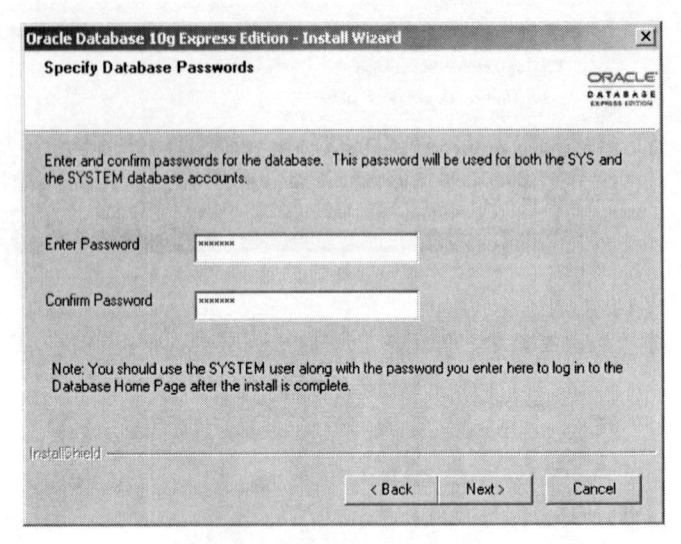

Figure 2: DBA Password

Don't forget the password you define here, you'll need it to perform most DBA type tasks such as creating users, starting/stopping the database and other administrative functions. If you forget the password, the easiest way to recover will be to repeat the install and thus create a new database.

Since the Oracle Express Edition installer also creates a starter database for you, this install process can take a while – so be patient. On a lesser power notebook this might take a half hour or more. That's normal.

Utilities

Once the Oracle Express Edition installer has completed, you'll find the following new application shortcuts under the Start menu -> Programs as shown here in Figure 3.

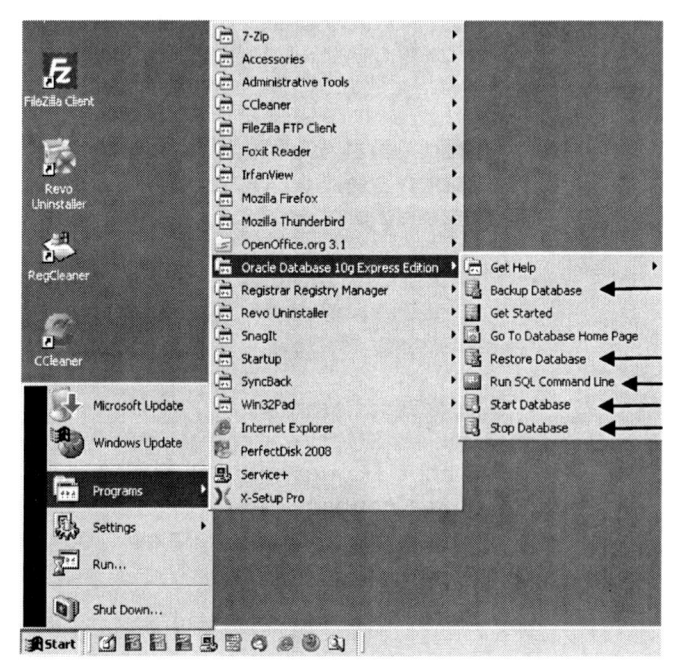

Figure 3: Oracle Express Programs

There are five programs worth note:

- "Backup Database" runs a command script that shuts down database and then backs it up

- "Restore Database" runs a command script that shuts down the database, restores it and then starts it back up

- "Start Database" runs a command script to start up the background database process

- "Shutdown Database" runs a command script to shut down the background database process

- "Run SQL Command Line" starts up Oracle's SQL*plus command interpreter without a connection, thus you must issue a connect system/your_install_password before you can do anything

Note that by default the Oracle Express Edition database is setup to automatically start both the network listener and database services during a windows boot. So your database will be available every time you start your PC as shown here in Figure 4 (the Windows Services Manager). You might want to change those two services to not start automatically to keep your PC boot time reasonable. You can always start the database when needed using the "Start Database" described above.

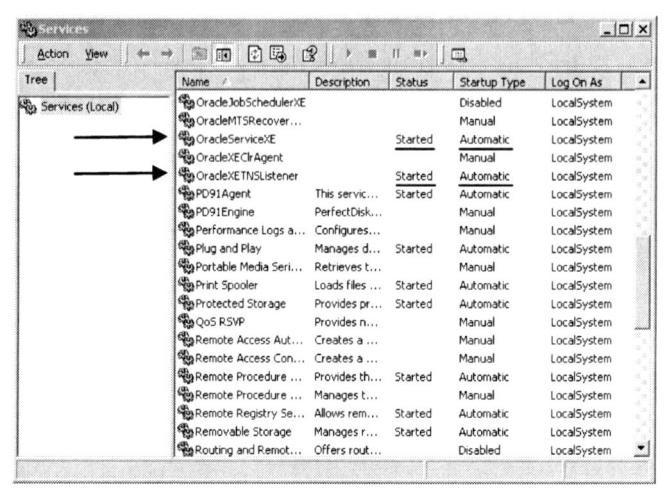

Figure 4: Oracle Windows Services

SQL Developer

Since Oracle Express Edition is based on Oracle 10g, it does not include SQL Developer – which did not come as part of the standard client and database install until Oracle 11g.

However SQL Developer will work just fine with Oracle Express Edition. You simply need to download the free SQL Developer zip file, place a shortcut on your desktop to the executable, and launch the application. For more details refer back to Chapter 7.

Conclusion

In this chapter we covered how to create an Oracle sandbox or playground for you to experiment with and not risk production data or interfering with other peoples' work. The Oracle Express Edition is totally free, offers all the database features of significance, and is fairly lightweight in terms of install space and computer resources consumed. Thus by working with your very own local Oracle database you can learn more and faster – and all with no worries.

Author Bio

Bert Scalzo is a Database Expert for Quest Software and a member of the TOAD dev team. He has worked with Oracle databases for well over two decades. Mr. Scalzo's work history includes time at both Oracle Education and Oracle Consulting. He holds several Oracle Masters certifications and an extensive academic background - including a **BS**, **MS** and **PhD** in Computer Science, an **MBA**, plus insurance industry designations. Mr. Scalzo is also an **Oracle ACE**. ♠

Mr. Scalzo is accomplished speaker and has presented at numerous Oracle conferences and user groups - including OOW, ODTUG,

IOUG, OAUG, RMOUG and many others. His key areas of DBA interest are Data Modeling, Database Benchmarking, Database Tuning & Optimization, "Star Schema" Data Warehouses, Linux and VMware.

Mr. Scalzo has written numerous articles, papers and blogs - including for the Oracle Technology Network (OTN), Oracle Magazine, Oracle Informant, PC Week (eWeek), Dell Power Solutions Magazine, The LINUX Journal, LINUX.com, Oracle FAQ, Ask Toad and Toad World.

Mr. Scalzo has also written eight books:
- Oracle DBA Guide to Data Warehousing and Star Schemas
- TOAD Handbook (1st Ed.)
- TOAD Handbook (2nd Ed.)
- TOAD Pocket Reference (2nd Ed.)
- Database Benchmarking: Practical Methods for Oracle & SQL Server
- Advanced Oracle Utilities: The Definitive Reference
- Oracle on VMware: Expert Tips for Database Virtualization
- Introduction to Oracle: Basic Skills for Any Oracle User